Managing Improvement

Managing Improvement

A Book Targeted to Help Middle Management Develop
and Implement a Holistic Approach to Driving
Continuous Improvement in Their Organizations

William G. Doak

iUniverse, Inc.
New York   Bloomington

Managing Improvement
A Book Targeted to Help Middle Management Develop and Implement a
Holistic Approach to Driving Continuous Improvement in Their Organizations

iUniverse books may be ordered through booksellers or by contacting:

iUniverse
1663 Liberty Drive
Bloomington, IN 47403
www.iuniverse.com
1-800-Authors (1-800-288-4677)

ISBN: 978-0-595-47907-8 (pbk)
ISBN: 978-0-595-71398-1 (cloth)

Printed in the United States of America

Contents

Preface

This book contains numerous charts, figures and tools for helping managers put in place the structures for implementing a system for driving improvement throughout their organizations. At first glance, all these tools and charts will seem overwhelming. It is important to understand that improvement is more a fundamental philosophy than any set of structures. Everyone in the organization needs to be striving to improve what they do.

Just start the process as simply as possible, and develop the structures as you go. You can start anywhere in the process, but probably the best place to start is at the annual review and by conducting a Situation Analysis.

History and Rationale for Managing Improvement

The Target Audience

This book is dedicated to middle management. By middle management, I mean those individuals who manage the bulk of the organization's people and resources and carry the primary responsibility for delivering quality products and services to their customers. In large organizations, these people are frequently called operations management or department managers. Although the information contained herein focuses on those whose primary responsibility is to provide products and services to paying customers; those who manage services internal to an organization and not-for-profit organizations will also find the information useful.

Many organizations have been through significant change over the last three decades. They were exposed to Total Quality Management (TQM) in the eighties, reengineering in the nineties, and in the new century, globalization. This has resulted in companies outsourcing the production of their products and services to third-world countries where the labour is much cheaper.

In spite of these tumultuous changes, there are still people and businesses trying to provide goods and services who must manage their resources in the most efficient and effective manner for their customers. It is to these people that I dedicate this book.

History of the Development of Managing Improvement

The development of this book is a result of my personal journey as an internal quality-management consultant to a large international company during the eighties and nineties.

The company I worked for was going through a painful experience as a result of the oil crisis and a subsequent economic downturn in the early eighties, and its leadership was frantically trying to find a solution to its poor financial returns. The manufacturing sector was leading the search, and various geographic locations were investigating some form of quality management in hopes of improving their profitability.

The division that I worked for was no different, and as a result of a change in leadership at my location, the new leader, who favoured a Deming approach to management, decided to introduce Statistical Quality Control (SQC) training to the site. The title chosen for this effort was Continuous Improvement. It soon became obvious that SQC was a tool and not a system. Those who had been trained did not understand how SQC was going to help them become more efficient. There was a need to structure teams and to develop a process for them to follow. This led to the development of the "Opportunity Flow Chart" (a team problem-solving process). This process was quite successful initially, but after a short time it became obvious that the teams lacked direction and frequently worked on things their supervisors did not support. This led to frustration both by the team members and their supervisors. The problem was that the people at the working level did not see a clear connection between their efforts and the organization's vision and goals. They did not see how this continuous improvement effort was going to help them make a difference.

It became obvious that something was missing. Both corporate business leadership and site management wanted improvement to happen, and they were providing what they thought were the tools employees needed to make them more effective and efficient. To compound this problem, there were numerous management gurus espousing a variety of different tools, processes and courses, such as Just In Time (JIT), quality function deployment, seven management tools, policy deployment and many others. Still, something was missing—something that would pull all of this together in an organized and strategic fashion.

The Journey towards Managing Improvement

GOAL/QPC, a quality-management research organization which was started in the late seventies and early eighties and funded by the local Boston-area business and public sector, had been researching the Japanese success story and publishing their findings. In 1987, the organization I worked for became a member of this organization. It was at this time that it began to become apparent that policy deployment (or "Managing by Planning," as the GOAL/QPC group called it) might present a solution for pulling all the quality-management tools and processes together into a coherent and focused system.

Over a two-year period, a course was put together entitled "Managing Improvement." It was presented to the middle management of the company. The course was very well received, and many departments succeeded in creating a more systematic and focused effort in driving continuous improvement in their departments.

Concerns about the Managing Improvement Course

Based on feedback from the participants, the original course was noted to be weak in areas such as:

- Developing clear departmental key-performance measures linked to the business-performance measures and stratified from the business through the department level and down to the natural work groups;
- Ensuring that training, reinforcement and support structures were in place for helping those involved in implementing tactics;
- Providing clear direction, support and progress reviews by team sponsors;
- Performing in-depth studies of what worked and what didn't work, with resultant recommendations at all levels, particularly at the leadership level;
- Sharing and replicating key learning across the organization.

What Has Been Incorporated into Managing Improvement?

Since retiring, I have continued to volunteer my experience and services to many other organizations. It has been my observation that the need by middle management for help in developing an understanding of, as well as methodologies for, developing effective and efficient organizations that drive continuous improvement and quality control is as great now as it was back in the eighties.

This has resulted in this book, in which I will provide a more thorough explanation of how to do a Situation Analysis. Better linkage has been made to the business strategy and daily management/quality control systems. In addition, information has been added on methodologies for ensuring that:

- All the components for a continuous improvement system are incorporated;
- Motivational and support plans and structures are in place so that people:
  - Know what is needed;

- Know how to develop and achieve tactics and plans;
- Are reinforced and supported when taking action.

What Do Some Experts Say, and What Has Industry's Experience Been in Terms of Continuous Improvement and Quality Management?

Continuous Improvement is more than "nice to have." In change and evolution lies the very survival of business organizations. In a TV series, Dr. Michael Porter, a well-known professor who teaches at MIT in Boston, argued that sustainable competitive advantage must be achieved through differentiation from the competition. Differentiation is the result of either inventing something that cannot be easily replicated, or by improving at a rate faster than the competition. In the author's view, inventing something that cannot be replicated by the competition, although possible in the short term, is extremely unlikely in the long term. Improving at a faster rate is a more effective strategy for maintaining the survival of an organization. (Michael Porter, 1985)

A few companies have been very successful in their application of Continuous Improvement and Total Quality Management. However, many other organizations who have dabbled in Continuous Improvement and TQM have abandoned them. Typical of the short-term thinking of North American managers, many organizations have moved on to other fads in hopes of finding the "magic bullet" that will help them to achieve a competitive advantage. In fact, change management poses a major challenge for most companies. Whatever the nature of the initiative, success rates are disturbingly poor.

- A. T. Kearney, in *The TQM Magazine*, found that 80 per cent of TQM initiatives fail to produce tangible results.
- An alliance between Business Intelligence and Templeton College's research into reengineering efforts found that as many as 90 per cent fail to produce breakthrough results.
- The research consultancy IDC suggests that the failure rate for all corporate change programs is around 70 per cent.
- The level of familiarity with strategic thinking in the U.S. is high, but acceptance is low. (Fred R. David, 1995)

  One obstacle is that top executives are often too busy fighting fires to devote time to developing managers who can think strategically. Yet, the best run companies recognize the need to develop managers who can fashion and implement strategy.

Resistance to change can be considered the single greatest threat to successful strategy implementation.

The Need for Managing Improvement Based on My Personal Experience

My experience at the company for which I worked, along with exposure to management literature (see bibliography) and to many speakers at a variety of management seminars, has convinced me that *implementation* of business strategy is a key issue for organizations. Selecting the right business strategy is, of course, a necessity, but getting it implemented is every bit as important. Middle management is key to making this happen. They have to know what is important to the business (measurably) and they have to know how to organize their resources to achieve business goals. *I have found Managing Improvement to be the fundamental process for helping middle management put in place a continuous improvement system that will allow for effective implementation of business strategies.*

Managing Improvement is about helping management to think strategically and to align and motivate people by involving them in the pursuit of the business vision and strategy.

Note: Some have suggested that middle management have resisted change because they feel threatened by it or simply do not want to change. This is not characteristic of department or operational managers with whom I have been associated. Most of the resistance, I have observed, results from a lack of understanding as to how all the many pieces of change fit together and how they are linked to the achievement of the business goals.

Why is the implementation of strategy and change so difficult? The reasons are many, but two of the key ones for organizations are: not taking a holistic or systems approach to change and Continuous Improvement (CI) and lack of constancy of purpose (an unwillingness to spend the time to learn and improve).

Holistic or Systems Approach to CI

Systems thinking and a systems approach to TQM was the theme of a GOAL/ QPC conference held in Boston in 1993. It was noted that many organizations had tried various parts of TQM approaches such as quality circles, Statistical Quality Control and customer-focus initiatives. Although gains had been made, most of these organizations were unable to maintain the momentum. Dr. Russell Ackoff, one of the keynote speakers at the conference and a leading authority on systems thinking, spoke about the need to understand systems thinking. In his opinion, *understanding* and *using* systems thinking was the most critical potential source of competitive advantage for North America in the coming years. In his book entitled *The Fifth Discipline*, Peter Senge explains how tools such as computer simulations, causal loop diagrams and system archetypes can be used as a means for analyzing the cause-and-effect relationships that occur within business organizations.

Most of the literature on strategy development and implementation is strong on strategy development and very weak on strategy implementation. *Managing Improvement* has been developed to fill the gap. In addition, the literature on business organizations typically deals with a reactive response to change and evolution. This reactive response involves trying to understand, and maybe even predict, the forces that may impinge on the business. This also assumes that management can make the appropriate responses that will allow the organization to survive. This is a problem-oriented approach, as opposed to an opportunity or visionary approach. A visionary approach is knowing where you want to be (now) and putting plans in place to take you there. This includes looking out into the future for possible scenarios that might derail your journey and putting in place contingencies for dealing with such scenarios.

Whichever approach is taken, leaders and managers must seek to understand the systems that are functioning within their organizations and take a proactive approach to optimizing their systems' performance. Managing Improvement is about a proactive approach to Continuous Improvement.

Constancy of Purpose (Spending the Time to Learn and Improve).

The last of Dr. Edwards Deming's well-known fourteen points from his book *The New Economics* (1993) was the need for constancy of purpose. One of his more famous quotes is, "There is no instant pudding." Deming was noted for his harshness in speaking to North American management, particularly in criticizing what he considered to be a failure to take the long-term view or to focus on meeting the needs of all organizational stakeholders (particularly the employees and customers).

Who Needs to Know and Use the Managing Improvement Process?

It was Deming who said that 85 per cent of the reasons why people do not do quality work relate to deficiencies within the system in which they work. (He later changed this to 95 per cent). He suggested that since managers control the organization's systems, it is their responsibility to change them (Deming, Edwards, 1993).

Although everyone in the organization needs to understand their roles in making Continuous Improvement happen, it is the department or operations leaders and managers who control the bulk of the organization's resources. In controlling both the people and equipment resources, they are also the prime spenders of capital and expense dollars. This is the group that must fully support and take a proactive stance in achieving the business goals.

Experience has shown that the "buck stops" at the middle-management or operational level. These people have enormous pressures and demands from the business leadership, from local government regulations, the public, employees and local customers. In addition, they have various requests for resources to work on initiatives sponsored by internal functional groups. As they frequently feel overwhelmed by these pressures, it was not surprising, at least in the company that I worked for, that the managers responded enthusiastically to Managing Improvement.

How Does Managing Improvement Fit with Other Systems within an Organization?

Dr. James Sprague, a retired professor who taught industrial engineering in the Mechanical Engineering Department at the University of Alberta, suggested that a business organization is primarily composed of three major systems. These systems are (1) setting the standard, (2) meeting the customer's requirements (delivering a quality product) and (3) Continuous Improvement.

Managing Improvement (MI) is an attempt to provide management with an understanding of what is required to implement a Continuous Improvement system. MI is intended to help ensure that management and the organization for which they are accountable is organized, aligned and continuously learning and improving towards the achievement of an organization's purpose or vision. Managing Improvement is a process that helps middle managers sort out these issues. It provides them with a means for focusing, and for telling them that they are in control.

What Is Managing Improvement?

Perfection will never be achieved. Managing Improvement is not a destination, but a journey. It is composed of:

- A strategic and organized approach to understanding and focusing on the needs of the organization's key stakeholders;
- A search to understand, optimize and use the fundamental forces of cause and effect that underlie the functioning of the organization;
- An attitude of constantly seeking for excellence in everything that is done;
- An alignment and motivation of everyone in the organization towards its overall purpose;
- A cycle of learning (plan, do, check and act) woven into the thoughts and structures of the organization at all levels.

What Managing Improvement Is Not

Managing Improvement is not a short-term fix. It is not limited to reengineering, process improvement, problem-solving teams, quality assurance, Just In Time, creativity or many of the other components associated with TQM. Nor is it simply about all the structures, training and documented processes that are put in place. It encompasses all of these and more. It is the system that managers and others work with on their evolutionary journeys towards their visions. It is proactive as opposed to reactive, and it requires that managers lead rather than react.

The Danger

Inherent to *Managing Improvement,* as with all other structures and processes that are incorporated into organizations, is the danger that it might become bureaucratic and inflexible. After all, this has become the mark of many strategic planning exercises. MI needs to be understood as a way of thinking, a set of values and an organized and dedicated approach to learning and finding ways of doing things better. Strategies change, and what may be important to focus on today may not be what the organization has to focus on tomorrow. The process has to be able to change rapidly to meet new and different needs as they occur. A breakthrough issue today may be an incremental or insignificant issue tomorrow. MI, by the very nature of its design, allows for adaptation to the organization's new situation.

The Managing Improvement Model

Managing Improvement is based on the fundamental "learning wheel," or the "Shewhart Cycle," as it is referred to by Deming (Deming, Edwards, 1993). This is the cycle or wheel of learning that is fundamental to all problem—or opportunity-resolution processes. The diagram below depicts the Managing Improvement model.

Fig. 1: The Fundamental, Five-Phase Model for Managing Improvement

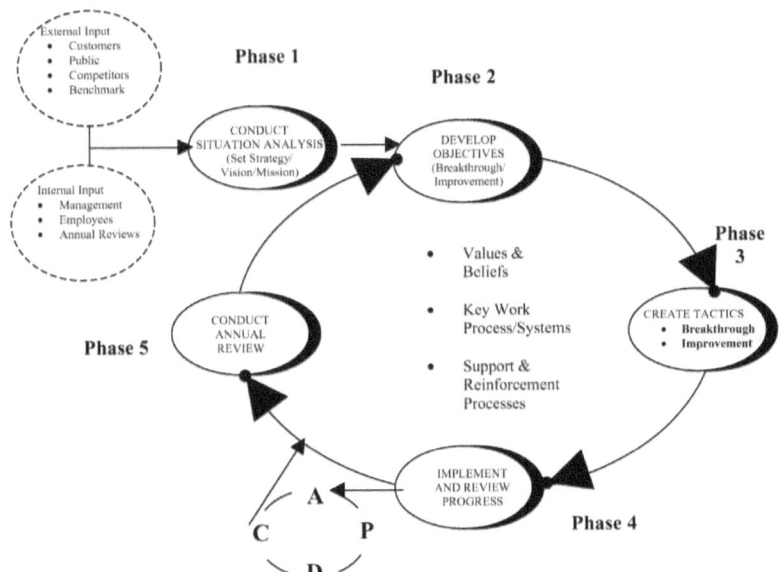

The Plan (P), Do (D), Check (C), Act (A) five-phase model is used at all levels of the organization, from the business leadership team, through the department or operational leadership team, to the project teams or natural work groups who implement the organization's plans.

It is the same fundamental process that is used by the business-management team and by project teams and natural work groups as they work to set goals and implement plans. These processes connect horizontally between groups at critical points, such as where input is required for developing strategy, for communicating the final business goals and reviewing of progress and recommendations for improvements.

The five-phase model is a process designed to help managers take a disciplined, proactive approach towards improvement in their areas of influence. The model provides a mechanism whereby managers and leaders, through disciplined reviews, can improve their ability to prioritize, as well as improve the way they plan, and accelerate improvements in the key performance areas for which they are accountable.

Overview and Summary of How Managing Improvement Works

MI is a cyclical learning model that managers work through on an annual basis. Its ultimate focus is on the organization's vision, but it also works to achieve that vision through the establishment of intermediate and long-term objectives. The purpose of the annual review cycle is to make sure that the strategies and tactics are still appropriate and that they are aligned with the business strategies and objectives. MI consists of five phases, which are briefly summarized below.

Phase One: Situation Analysis

In this phase, an in-depth examination of the external and internal factors affecting the organization's performance occurs. This is called a Strengths, Weaknesses, Opportunities and Threats (SWOT) analysis. Competitor analysis and benchmarking of the best in class are key inputs to this phase. From this analysis, the vision and mission is developed, along with key performance measures. This is a one-time exercise which establishes the data-collection structures. Once completed, the Situation Analysis phase becomes part of the annual review process. This usually occurs in the second cycle of using the Managing Improvement process.

Phase Two: Develop Objectives

In this phase, potential breakthrough objectives are identified. Also, the departments are asked to identify the incremental improvements they are working on and what impact they will have on the organization's key performance areas.

Phase Three: Create Tactics

Creating plans at this level of management is about developing strategies and tactics which have to be achieved in order to attain the breakthrough objectives identified in phase two. Once the tactics are firm, the target and time frame for the objectives are confirmed. In addition, the organization is asked to communicate the goals in place for improving the organization's key performance measures. These goals are then rolled up, and annual improvement targets are set.

Phase Four: Implement and Review Progress

Implementation and review is about communicating the annual improvement plan, establishing feedback systems, implementing appropriate training, establishing support structures and supporting and reinforcing appropriate behaviours.

Phase Five: Annual Review

Once the Managing Improvement process is in place, this phase replaces the situation analysis phase. Results are reviewed, competitor and benchmark comparisons are made, and an internal and external situation analysis is conducted. The knowledge from this analysis is incorporated into the Managing Improvement process in order to make it perform better in the coming year. After this phase, the process starts all over again, with finer improvements occurring year after year.

Evaluation of the Impact of MI

The most obvious desired result of the implementation of Managing Improvement is the achievement of the business goals—usually financial goals. Business people frequently refer to this as "bottom-line" measurement. To achieve the business goals, middle managers must achieve their goals. Bottom-line measures tell how the business has done but do not necessarily tell how it will do in the future (lagging measures). Other measurements (leading measures) are indicators of future performance and are also important to a well-implemented improvement process. On evaluating the effectiveness of Managing Improvement, managers should look for the following outcomes:

- Maintenance and improvement in key stakeholder satisfaction other than just the shareholders—in particular, how satisfied the paying customer is;
- Improvement in process performance;
- Improvement in the ability of employees to maintain and improve performance in their areas of responsibility.

Conclusion

Managing Improvement provides a disciplined approach for managers to follow. It will help managers focus and align their areas of responsibility towards the needs of the business. It is intended to provide an overall *business-focused, systemic and organized approach by everyone towards continuous performance improvement.*

The Nature

Of

Change

The Nature of Change

Change can seem very threatening to people. For some, it is extremely difficult. In the author's experience, people are not afraid of change, but they are very resistant to being changed. What this means is that when people feel they have some control over change, it is less threatening to them.

Management needs to understand people's reaction to change and identify ways to help overcome their natural resistance to it.

People's Reaction to Change

There are two ways people in an organization undergo change: *reactionary* or *visionary* (Berger and Sikora 1994).

Reactionary is the more passive role, wherein people within an organization respond to an external stimulus and, in general, feel pretty helpless. They tend to think they are subject to the dictates of what is going on around them.

Visionary is the more active role, wherein people within an organization have a clearer vision of where they want to go and what they want to become. A visionary organization identifies what it wants to be or look like, and then sets in place strategies to get them there. It also identifies contingencies for overcoming obstacles which might prevent them from getting there. This generally leads to a more positive attitude in the organization and a feeling of being in control and involved.

Proactive or Visionary Model

It is the visionary or proactive change agents (managers) for whom this training is targeted; hence the title *Managing Improvement*. Improvement is not limited to management, but involves the whole organization. It requires a strong visionary leader who, as Stephen Covey says, "Climbs the ladder in order to see in which direction the organization should be going" (Covey, Stephen, 1991—see bibliography). Then, after determining the correct direction (vision), the leader needs to align and support the organization with the appropriate leadership in order to help the organization most efficiently move in the direction of its vision.

3

Introduction

Although change is inevitable, this does not mean that we, as individuals or as organizations, must remain passive in response to it.

The Hierarchy of Change

Introduction

Managing Improvement is about change. Not all levels in an organization are equally involved in their time commitments to change. It is vitally important that the upper levels of management take a lead role in making change happen. In fact, at the top level of the organization, close to 100 per cent of the leader's time should be spent in trying to focus and align the organization towards outstanding performance.

Types and Levels of Change within an Organization

At the top of an organization, the focus on change or improvement is at a *strategic* and *visionary* level (what and where). As we move down the organization, change or improvement becomes more *tactical* in regard to how to make the change happen (how and when).

This move from strategic to tactical is reflected in the diagram below, which shows the proportion of time that would or should be spent on the various change processes depending on the management level in the organization.

Fig. 2: Appropriate Modes or Processes of Change as it Relates to the Level of Management and to the Amount of Time Management Needs to Spend on Change

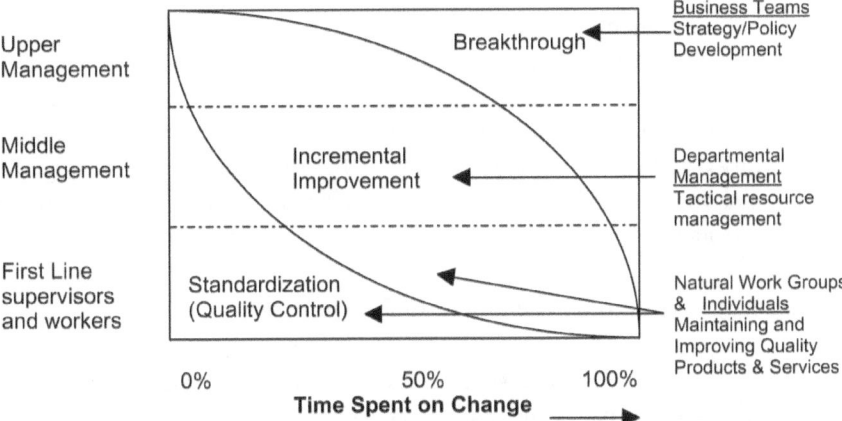

In this period of rapid change, management needs structured systems that focus on using a variety of modes and processes of change that enhance the rate of improvement. It is not a question of whether organizations have to change to be competitive. They must change at an ever-increasing rate that allows them to out-pace their competition, or at the very least match them.

The Three Sub-processes Involved in Managing Improvement and Change

Breakthrough involves more radical change in an organization and usually crosses various functions. It means reinventing or radically altering present processes. As the name suggests, this process involves discontinuous change, as opposed to incremental change, in parts of, or all of, the organization. The higher up in the organization the breakthrough process is used, the less collaborative and more directive it becomes.

Incremental improvement involves small changes which, although collectively able to result in a breakthrough for the organization, are more likely to be changes that occur at the working level. The management of incremental improvement involves the middle levels of the organization, where project teams and individuals are focused on making a breakthrough at their level. This process requires a much more collaborative approach.

Standardization (quality control) is notoriously left out of the change process in North American organizations. It is the process which ensures that both the break-through and incremental improvements are institutionalized by means of creating new control systems or modifying existing ones. Without standardization and control, the benefits of change are very quickly lost or reduced. A misconception in regard to standardization is that it is at odds with change or improvement. When standardization is appropriately applied, it is an essential component of change or improvement. Standardization is really about the transfer of continuous improvement to quality control. It is about making sure that the appropriate training, documentation and accountability are in place for the new standards of performance. The ISO 9000 standards are about standardization and quality control.

Managing Improvement as the Overall Change Process

In many organizations, the processes of change are not well understood or actively focused on. Consequently, change happens more by chance than by plan. In addition, the gains that are made are frequently lost due to a lack of standardization and process control.

Managing Improvement is intended to be the overall process by which change is orchestrated throughout an organization. It provides the discipline for the PDCA (plan, do, check and act) cycle that is fundamental to any improvement system. MI ensures a structured and systematic approach by which an organization can achieve its goals. *Another way of depicting Managing Improvement is to say that it follows the PDCA, or cycle of learning model, through which personal and organizational performance can be improved.*

Fig. 3: The Deming Cycle, or Shewhart Cycle (PDCA)

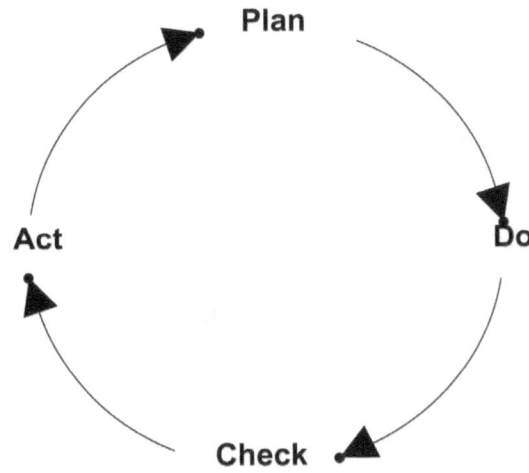

Effect of the Traditional Ways of Improving Versus the Effect of the Proactive Ways of Doing Improvement

Fig. 4: Typical Organizational Improvement over Time, as Compared to a Focused Improvement Effort

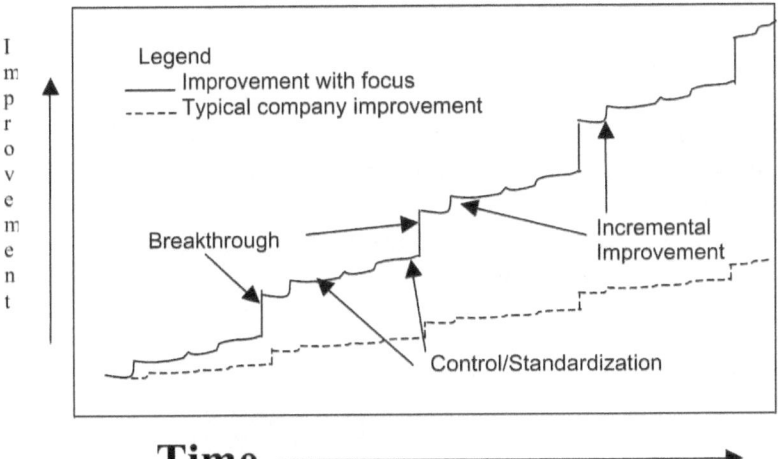

Values, Beliefs and Change

Introduction

In order for change to become an integral part of the culture of an organization and for *Managing Improvement* to function efficiently, certain underlying assumptions must be held by the majority of the people working in the organization, particularly those who manage it. These underlying assumptions can be broken down into values and beliefs. These must be in alignment with the principles that define the laws of cause and effect and underlie the functioning of any organization or system. Understanding these principles (cause and effect) is at the heart of optimizing an organization's performance and achieving a sustainable advantage.

Definitions

Principles The ultimate source, origin or cause of something; a fundamental truth, law, doctrine or motivating force, upon which other laws or doctrines are based. Understanding principles is the basis of Continuous Improvement, as a constant search for cause-and-effect relationships is fundamental to making sustainable improvements.

Values Something important to an individual; something considered worthy of possessing or appreciating. Values that are at odds with principles will eventually lead to conflict within an organization, and ultimately to less than its optimal performance. It is important to value principles.

Beliefs A mental model or way of thinking about how things work—frequently so ingrained that it does not appear at the conscious level of thinking. Since beliefs are so ingrained and seldom questioned, they have been found to be one of the key barriers to making progress in an organization. It is important to surface and challenge these beliefs or assumptions on an ongoing basis.

Principles and Beliefs

Principles are usually learned through experience (a cause-and-effect relationship exists). The law of gravity, for example, has come to be accepted as a fundamental principle, since experience has determined that when something is thrown up in the air, it invariably falls down. It has become our belief that in all cases that when something is thrown up, it will invariably fall down. When an instance occurs that this is not the case, then our belief (theory or mental model) is challenged, and further study is conducted to see if there is a more fundamental principle which will cover both the case when the thrown object falls down and when it does not. Principles and beliefs go hand-in-hand. First, there is the belief that when something is thrown up, it will fall down. After a large body of experience is gathered and many attempts are made to disprove this belief, it eventually gets accepted as a law or a fundamental principle (that this is always the case—objects, when thrown up, do fall down).

There is a body of experience gradually being gathered that suggests certain values and beliefs are fundamental to the implementation of a continuous improvement system. These basic principles are fundamental to the optimal performance of an organization that seeks to provide long-term value to its key stakeholders. These principles will be referred to as "guiding principles." They originate from the "quality principles" as espoused by the National Quality Institute of Canada.

Guiding Principles

The following principles are considered fundamental to any organization trying to implement effective and efficient continuous improvement. Note: The italicized and bulleted additional material came from a survey of government and business organizations, independently conducted by the author. The findings support the fact that these principles are considered to be important.

Quotes are from the booklet entitled *Canadian National Quality Institute Quality Principles*, 1996.

Cooperation, Teamwork and Partnering

Teamwork, in the spirit of cooperation rather than competition for individual gain, is nurtured and recognized. Cooperation, within and between organizations and inside and outside sector borders, is a cornerstone for the development of win-win relationships.

- *Cooperation and collaboration is valued (between departments, customers, suppliers, and others);*
- *Maximizing the development of the organization is valued more than maximizing personal power and status;*
- *There is a culture wherein there is a passion to listen and to understand others.*

Leadership through Involvement and by Example

Developing a quality approach involves a transformation in management thinking and behaviour at all levels. This can only be achieved by the active involvement of senior management to facilitate, reinforce and strive to exceed the needs of customers.

Primary Focus on Customers

In order to achieve goals, the primary aim of everyone in the organization must be to fully understand, meet and strive to exceed the needs of customers.

- *There is a culture that is focused on the customer (the people who pay);*
- *There is a culture wherein there is a passion to listen and to understand others.*

Respect for the Individual and Encouragement for People to Develop Their Full Potential

Critical for quality improvement are the values that impact the development of mutual respect between people that work in the organization; communication and personal development are directly related to these values. "People feel like they are contributing."

- *Growth and development of people is sought;*
- *There is a work environment that allows people to plan, do, check and act;*

- *Improve their own work (people are empowered);*
- *There is a culture wherein there is a passion to listen and to understand others.*

Contribution of Each and Every Individual

The aim is to give everyone, at all levels of the organization, the opportunity to use their creativity and to make a positive contribution to the organization's pursuit of excellence.

- *Everyone is encouraged to contribute to the maximum of their potential;*
- *There is a culture wherein people enjoy their work (high employee involvement).*

A Process-oriented and Prevention-based Strategy

An organization is a network of interdependent value-adding processes. Improvement is achieved through changing these processes to improve the total system. Managing by focusing on results alone is fruitless, since results are determined by the system in use. If the system is not changed in a fundamental way, the results will not improve. To facilitate long-term improvements, a mindset of prevention (versus correction) must be applied to eliminate the root causes of errors and waste.

Continuous Improvement of Methods and Outcomes

No matter how much improvement has been accomplished, there are always practical ways of doing better and of providing improved service or products to the customer.

- *Learning from others is valued (the belief or saying "not invented here" is not part of the culture);*
- *There is a culture where employees always strive for excellence;*
- *Admitting mistakes and learning from them is valued.*

Factual Approach to Decision Making

Decisions are made based upon measured data and an understanding of the cause-and-effect mechanisms at work, not simply on the basis of instinct, authority, or anecdotal data.

- *There is a fact based-decision-making culture;*
- *Constructive criticism is valued and sought;*
- *People are disciplined in their approach to solving problems and achieving excellence.*

Obligations to and Expectations of Stakeholders, Including an Exemplary Concern for and Responsibility to Society

An organization is seen as part of society, with important responsibilities to satisfy the expectations of its people, customers, suppliers and all stakeholders.

- *There is a culture wherein there is a high degree of honesty and integrity;*
- *There is a balance between the business needs and the employee needs.*

The Paradox (Competition versus Collaboration)

An issue that runs at the core of the guiding principles is collaboration versus competition. Which one achieves optimum performance for the organization? Like many seemingly incompatible paradoxes, the answer is not either/or, but also/and. Competition is a fundamental driving force for change—it is ever present and will not allow either individuals or organizations to rest in the status quo. On the other hand, any system or organization trying to optimize its performance cannot have competition occurring between its subsystems or functional groups. These subsystems must collaborate to achieve the optimum for the overall system or organization. To illustrate this point, imagine the effect of the stomach deciding it wanted a greater share of blood and energy and taking it from the heart or the brain. The stomach might perform better, but the person as a whole would perform less efficiently.

Management must decide who or what lies within the core of the organization and when collaboration and cooperation are appropriate. The crux of this decision occurs with the decision on how to treat the employees. Are they to be involved in achieving the business goals, or are they just a cost to the organization, and therefore to be used and discarded as the occasion dictates? More and more organizations are finding that they have to broaden their perception of the collaborative system they work in, and they are inviting suppliers and distributors to be part of their system.

It may be that the factors involved in optimizing the whole are so complex that it is not possible for individuals to anticipate all the consequences of their actions. Therefore, they must rely on looking after the interests of the most obvious stakeholders and building in flexible systems to ensure that the other special-interest stakeholders have a chance to have their concerns heard and addressed.

Core Belief Principle(s)

It is a core belief of the author that seeking to optimize the good of the whole (system) versus sub-optimizing certain portions will in actuality achieve the maximum benefit not only to the whole but to the individual parts as well.

Key Processes or Subsystems

In order to optimize the potential for the success of implementing *Managing Improvement,* there are three subsystems (discussed earlier) that must be in place: catchball (a communication and feedback system), cross-functional management and quality control.

Catchball

Catchball refers to the commitment to continual communication that is essential to the development of realistic targets and the means to their deployment at every level of the company. Feedback systems must be put in place to break down linear communication flows and allow for bottom-up, top-down, horizontal, multi-directional communication, about targets, means, and their deployment progress. In order to establish such a communication system there must already be in the company, a commitment to total employee involvement and an understanding of the crucial role each employee plays in the continuous improvement process. (Akao 1991)

Cross-functional Management

Cross-functional management refers to the establishment of teams or management structures where there are defined accountabilities within a company for managing improvement in certain key areas of focus. These are usually the strategic areas defined in a company's vision or mission such as: quality, cost, delivery, safety and environment. Management teams which are constructed at various levels within an organization have the mandate to ensure that these strategic areas are managed cross-functionally. The same PDCA (Managing Improvement process) is used by the cross-functional teams as is used by the business management team. (Akao 1991)

Daily Management (Quality Control)

Maintaining quality products and services or meeting customer requirements is integral to daily management. Daily Management is the establishment of control systems within the organization such that consistency is ensured in the output of all the key processes within the organization. This involves identification of customers, performance measures (process and output) and accountabilities for the measurement and standardization of procedures and guidelines.

Quality Control

Meeting Customer Requirements

Introduction

Meeting the customer's requirements for consistent and dependable quality can only be achieved through a well-documented quality control system and a management that ensures that there is a disciplined approach to following standards. However, quality control can not be static, as customer requirements are ever changing and standards must constantly improve. Standards can only be improved and met through a thorough understanding of cause and effect. As Dr. Edward Deming said, "It is not the employees who make defects in quality; it is the system within which they work."

Quality control is fundamental to daily management. In fact, for the most part they can be thought of as one and the same thing, particularly if quality control is broadened to encompass all key aspects of an organization's business and not just those processes that deliver quality products and services.

For Managing Improvement to function, it must have a firm quality control foundation. In this case, quality control means *having all the performance measures, processes, accountabilities, standards and procedures documented and being used in order to assure that customer requirements are met.*

The European ISO 9000 standards provide an example of one quality control system that focuses on ensuring the consistency and dependability of the product or service that is being delivered. It is important to note that meeting the ISO standards does not necessarily ensure quality—it only ensures consistency.

The Japanese have founded quality control (QC) on Statistical Quality Control (SQC) and Statistical Process Control (SPC) tools, and in addition have expanded the concept of QC to include improvement by *focusing on root-cause analysis through the use of statistical tools.*

Many Japanese companies have expanded quality control to all the important performance areas within an organization, not just to the quality of the product or service delivered. For example, safety, environment and delivery are also included in quality control. Quality control means quality in all aspects of the business.

Definitions

According to the Japanese Industrial Standards (Z8101–1981) definition, quality control is a "system of means to economically produce goods or services that satisfy customer requirements."

When QC was first introduced to Japan by Deming in 1950, the main emphasis was on improving product quality by applying statistical tools in the production processes.

In 1954, J. M. Juran introduced the concept of QC as a vital management tool for improving managerial performance. Today, QC is used as a tool to build a system of continuing interaction among all elements responsible for the conduct of a company's business so as to achieve the improved quality that satisfies the customer's demand.

Thus, the term QC, as used in Japan, is almost synonymous with *kaizen*. Although the use of statistics remains its mainstay, QC has come to add many other tools, such as new seven new tools for improvement (Imai 1986).

Under the expanded definition, which also includes improvement, there are two main components of quality control. They are (1) control systems and (2) data gathering and analysis tools (which provide feedback for control, for understanding cause and effect and for making improvements).

Control System

Quality Control System Attributes

A quality control system has attributes similar to any other system. The primary objectives of a quality control system are: (1) to ensure that the performance measures, as decided by the key stakeholders concerned, are consistent and reliable and (2) to meet the agreed-upon requirements and time frame defined by the key stakeholders. The key attributes of a quality control system are:

The *customers* (their requirements)
The *supplier* (quality control)
The *processes* by which the inputs are transformed into outputs
The *process owners*
Indicators (measures of performance).
Targets
Standards and procedures

Customer	Every process has a customer who receives its output. It is important that it be understood who these people are and what they require.
Supplier	In addition to the customer, there are also inputs to the process. It is important to know who the key suppliers are and what impact they have on meeting the needs of the customer. There also needs to be quality control on the key delivered supplies.
Processes	A process is the sequence by which work gets done. It has inputs that are transformed into outputs as a result of work in progress throughout this process.
	There are multiple levels to processes, ranging from how the work gets done at the lowest level of the job, to the macro level of how customer needs are translated into new product design, to manufacture and delivery.
	Understanding and controlling how work gets done (the process) is *fundamental* to ensuring quality and making improvements.

Fig. 5: Diagram Showing Three Process Levels

1. Top Level
Macro Business Process

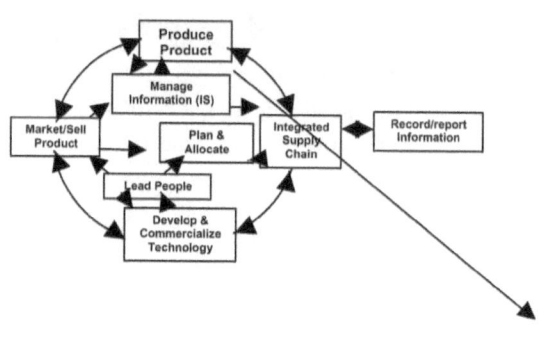

2 Mid-Level
Produce Product

3. Operation Level Operate Plant
   Process

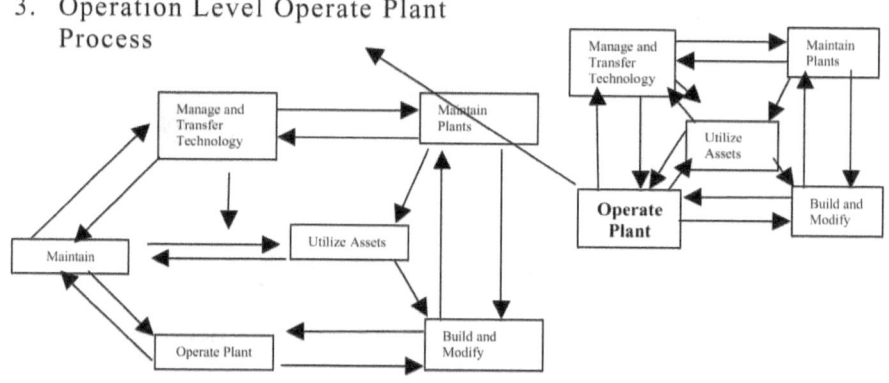

Process Owner The one who is ultimately accountable for the quality and quantity of the output of the process. In addition, such an individual is accountable for ensuring continuous improvement in the outputs of the process, as well as for improving the efficiency of the process itself.

Indicators There are essentially two kinds of measures within a control system:

- Quality indicators (QIs). These measure the performance of the outputs of the process as perceived by the customer.

These are the indicators for which the process owner is ultimately accountable.

- Process indicators (PIs). These measure important upstream steps in the process which have proven themselves to be key factors in affecting the performance of the quality indicators (QIs). Most processes are cross-functional, and the *points* of concern for PIs usually occur when there is a handover from one group or function to another.

Note: The QIs of one organizational level are usually the PIs of the next level up.

Targets   Targets are the expected level of performance for the QIs and PIs.

Standards and Procedures

Standards define the boundaries within which those who operate the process are confined. For example, the company may have decided that quality comes before quantity. Therefore, when the group arrives at a decision point between meeting the production demand QI and the quality QI, they will pursue quality first.

Procedures, on the other hand, are a documentation of the methodologies on how work gets done. As improvements are constantly being pursued, these will constantly be changing.

Fig. 6: A Diagram of the Elements of a Control System

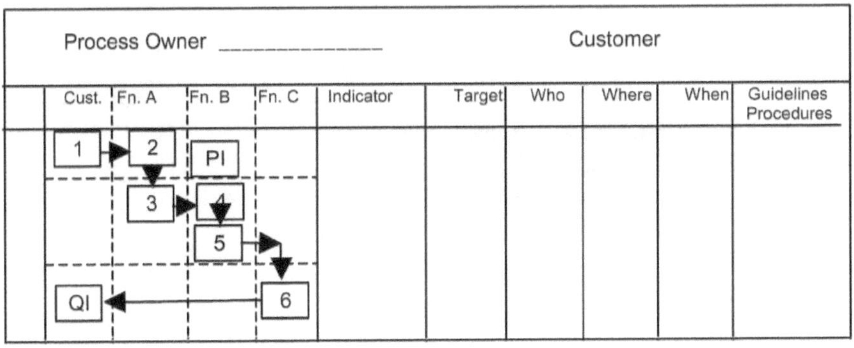

Data Gathering and Analysis Tools

Introduction Achieving a fundamental understanding of the forces of cause and effect that operate within a system is essential to making sustainable improvements. There are a number of tools which help in gathering and analyzing data, the most notable of which are those used in the discipline of statistics. These tools are excellent when it comes to understanding what has occurred in the past, but tend to fall short when trying to predict any distance into the future. To have longer-term predictability a model or theory which explains what is actually occurring at a fundamental level is required. It is from these models that one can predict what will happen in the future.

Quality control occurs after gaining an understanding of the cause-and-effect forces operating within a system, manipulating them to gain optimum performance, and putting in place control points with feedback to ensure the maintenance of desired levels of performance.

To understand these variables and their cause-and-effect relationship, there are a number of system analysis tools. A few of these are (1) seven quality control tools, (2) antecedent-behaviour-consequence (A-B-C) analysis and (3) system archetypes, as outlined by Peter Senge in *The Learning Organization*.

Seven Quality Control Tools

The most familiar tools for data gathering and analyzing for cause and effect are the seven quality control (QC) tools and other, more in-depth analysis tools, such as "design of experiments" and regression analysis.

The seven QC tools are:

- Check sheet
- Pareto charts
- Cause-and-effect diagram (fishbone or Ishikawa chart)

- Histogram
- Control chart
- Graphs
- Scatter diagram

Although the seven QC tools are familiar to most North American businesses, a fundamental understanding of the systems and attitudes that must be in place in order to make effective use of them is generally missing.

Antecedent-Behaviour-Consequence Analysis Model

A-B-C analysis is a model or theory which helps in understanding why people do the things they do. The underlying principle behind this model is the assumption that people do that which they find reinforcing to them. That is, behaviour continues because the performer receives a positive experience. The antecedent, which is the trigger for initiating behaviour, may get people to do something once. However, it is the ongoing positive or negative consequence to the individual that will cause the behaviour to continue or discontinue. This analysis is useful in trying to understand why people do what they do, and is also useful in helping to put together a plan to provide positive consequences that will encourage them to do what is key to optimizing the performance of an organization.

System Archetypes

See Peter Senge's book (1990) *The Learning Organization* for further details.

There are many tools available which can be used to understand the cause-and-effect forces that are in action within any system. The truly important point to be made here is that no system can be improved, optimized or controlled if the fundamental principles under which the system operates are not well understood.

Motivation

and Support

Elements Required to Motivate and Support People's Efforts to Improve

Introduction

It is truly amazing, in most organizations, how little management understands the impact that their actions have in creating attitudes and behaviours amongst their employees. It is perhaps unfair to single out managers in regard to this fault, as this ignorance extends to most of society. One has only to look at the issues that arise in parenting to see this. This is partly due to ignorance and partly due to an unwillingness to put in the time necessary to reinforce what their employees are doing. Managers truly need to develop a better understanding of what motivates people and to implement same if they wish to have an exemplar organization in which Managing Improvement can thrive.

In the author's opinion, for the majority of employees, it is intrinsically motivating to be recognized by themselves, by their peers, and by management for performing quality work and making improvements. In order to achieve this, the system within which employees operate must provide the reinforcement and support necessary to assist the achievement of these outcomes.

Strategies and tactics for providing motivational support fall primarily into seven categories or elements of change. Many of the thoughts for this section are taken from the book entitled *Performance Management R⁺* (Daniels 1989). Below is a summary of the elements of change to ensure that people are motivated and involved:

Seven key elements of change for ensuring that people are motivated and involved:

Improvement Culture

A *culture* that supports people's *intrinsic motivation* to do a good job.

Clearly Defined Results

A clear destination—a *vision* with *measureable goals*.

People Know How to Achieve the Results

Appropriate *training, job aids* **and** clearly defined *expectations* for those doing the work.

A Supportive System

Proactive management that identifies and *eliminates systemic barriers* and *provides support structures* such that people can do good work.

Feedback System

A well-developed *feedback system* that allows people to understand and know how they are progressing.

Reinforcement and Support Plan

A well-thought-out, positive *plan to shape and reinforce* the organizational skills and knowledge necessary to operate in the new system.

Flexible Implementation Process

An *implementation process* that takes into account that everything is changing. People need *time to adjust* to change, and constant *reviews and adjustments* to the plan are necessary to achieving the goal.

Improvement Culture

In order for an improvement culture to flourish, quality work and employee involvement must be valued in the organization. Very few managers would disagree that technical people need to be involved in improvement activities. But how many actually provide the time and resources for the "workers" to be involved in improvement teams, or in implementing innovative improvements they have suggested? Would such activities be encouraged or discouraged in your organization?

It is important that those in charge of the resources within an organization discuss and challenge their values and beliefs about employee involvement in improvement. A good starting point is the *quality principles* advocated by the National Quality Institute discussed earlier in the section on the nature of change.

Clearly Defined Results

In order to be effectively involved in improvement, employees need to know the ultimate destination. What is to be improved, and how would they know that it happened? The problem is that the expected results at the business level are often not meaningful to those at the working level. For example, often a worker does not know what he or she needs to do in order to increase market share.

It is important to understand that there is a hierarchy of results. The ultimate goal is to achieve those results which are important to the business and the organization as a whole. These results need to be defined at the level of every process and job so that they are meaningful to the people who are doing the work. This requires root-cause analysis and the use of the Pareto principle. The seven QC tools discussed earlier are important in this Pareto analysis.

Clearly Defined Results (cont.)

Fig. 7: Stratification of Business Objectives

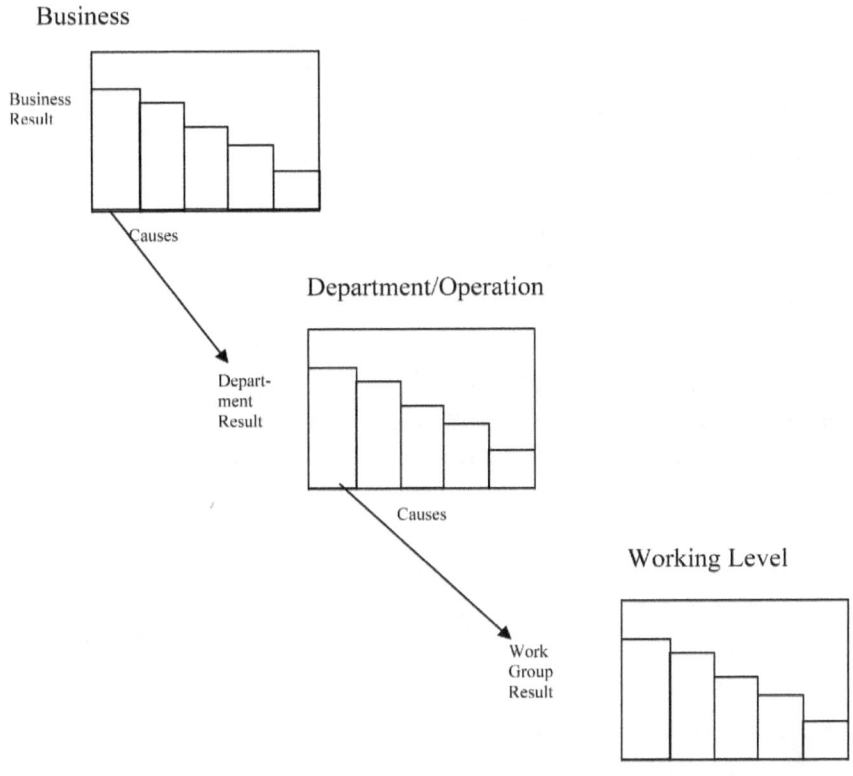

People Know How to Achieve the Results

Although it is important for employees to know what it is that they are trying to achieve (the result), it is equally important to have the skills and knowledge to be able to achieve the results (that is, how to get there). This involves:

a) Knowledge of their work area (for example, clerical office work)

b) Knowledge of where to get help

c) Skills and competence to make the necessary improvements

d) A process for making improvements

e) Guidelines for what they can and cannot do

A Supportive System

The people who have control of the resources (management) have to take a proactive stance in encouraging employee involvement and in removing barriers which prevent employees from being involved in improvement initiatives.

This could include:

- The ability to commit the organization's resources (for example, signing authority to purchase material or committing people's time to do work)

- Freedom to ask for help or support from other functions or technical resources

- Training in problem solving and root-cause analysis

- Time to pursue improvements

Feedback System

Defining the desired result and then ensuring that people get feedback on how they are progressing can be the two most significant components of an improvement system. Feedback has two components: (1) informing people on progress against the desired result and (2) informing individuals on their personal performance (skills and knowledge). The first component, feedback on progress towards a goal or measurable result, is usually straightforward and can occur by means of graphs or charts. The second component, getting feedback on one's personal performance in regard to the application of knowledge and skills, is not as straightforward. It usually involves the opinion of knowledgeable people. It is important that this feedback be as specific as possible and be presented in a manner that is perceived as being constructive.

Reinforcement and Support Plan

A system that is highly supportive and motivational takes a lot of commitment and effort to develop and implement. This is particularly true when something has changed or a change is being requested. Those who control the resources of an organization need to take a proactive stance in deciding how they will make this happen.

Note: Understanding what motivates people and building systems which will support motivation is not a simple matter of "common sense." Knowledge and skills in this area are notoriously weak in most organizations. Relevant training for management in understanding motivation is highly recommended for those trying to implement improvement systems.

Fig. 8: A Reinforcement Plan Guide

Performer _____ Measurable Result _____			
Key Behaviours	What will I do to ensure success	How will I reinforce the behaviours	F/I*
Plans to celebrate results			
Goals and Sub-Goals		Celebration for Meeting Goals and Sub-Goals	

F/I stands for Future/Immediate and is a reference to understanding whether the reinforcement will occur sometime after the behaviour occurs, or immediately after or during the behaviour. Immediate reinforcement is much more powerful than future reinforcement.

Creating a reinforcement or support plan involves developing a plan for change. This will require a kick-off or communication plan, (a one-time event) followed by many communication and review sessions (catchball) which set the stage for the change.

The following are some of the things that need to be considered in a kick-off or communication plan:

Kick-off or Communication Plan
- What to communicate
- Whom to communicate to
- When to communicate
- Where to communicate
- How to communicate
- Who will do the communicating
- Response or feedback expected from those being communicated to

Materials and Supplies Needed
- Overheads
- Audiovisual equipment
- Flipcharts

Barriers to Be Removed
- Identify what resistance may be encountered and what preventions or interventions might be appropriate to overcome this resistance.

Additional Training Needed
- What additional skills and knowledge may be required by those being communicated to in order for them to implement the organizational changes?

Miscellaneous

- Other things that may not have been previously been considered.

Flexible Implementation Process

It is important to understand that plans seldom go the way they were originally intended. It takes time for people to accept change and become part of it. Attention must be given to the normal emotional responses that people have to change. People tend to go through five stages. First there is *denial* (this, too, will pass); then *anger* (outright resistance); *bargaining* (if you do this, then I'll do that); *depression*; and, finally, *acceptance* (Dr. Elizabeth-Ross, 1996). The more people have been given a chance to be involved in planning the change, the shorter the period of resistance and the sooner and more likely there will be acceptance.

Note: Structured and detailed plans are less important than ensuring that everyone understands the goals (at their level) that must be achieved. Flexibility in how the goals are to be achieved is essential to ultimately achieving the goals. It is seldom possible to attain a goal through the application of any one method. It is likely that those involved in improvement will have to employ more than one action to achieve success. Again, the more important part of the process is communication of desired results and ensuring that people are supported and reinforced for achieving them.

"Planning is everything: plans are nothing," according to Thomas S. Axworthy (*National Post*, May 2006)

Key Roles in a Continuous Improvement System

Introduction   As in any system, certain key roles will have a significant impact on the performance of the system.

Key Roles

The following have been observed to be some of the key roles involved in an improvement system:

- Leadership
- Cross-functional leadership teams
- Operational leadership teams
- Project teams
- Natural work groups
- Technical support
- Process coach (someone knowledgeable in the change process who can lead the team through it)
- Personal coach (someone who helps individuals become the best they can be).

Purpose of Defining Roles

The purpose of defining roles is to ensure that individuals have clearly identified accountabilities and outcomes for which they are responsible. Without defining accountabilities, the achievement of the result is highly unlikely. People like to know what their roles are and how they will be evaluated by themselves and others.

Teams are an important structure for ensuring that action takes place. However, teams are not accountable for success; individuals are. It has been my experience that if you make more than one person accountable for the same result, then you have no one accountable. It needs to be understood that the group leader shares a greater responsibility for ensuring that action is taken. Team members are responsible for actively participating.

For teams to be successful, the members have to understand their roles on the team. They must have a process to follow and a team leader to lead them through it.

Leadership

Leadership is a quality that is needed by all people within an organization. Leadership is not about going off in one's own direction. It has to do with individuals taking charge and being proactive in trying to help the business achieve its vision and mission.

Leadership starts at the top of the organization through setting the organization's vision, mission and strategy, and the performance measures by which its progress will be assessed. Leaders then ensure that a) everyone understands what these goals are; b) ongoing communication is in place such that performance can be assessed; and c) they can ensure that the support and resources are available for those who need them.

Cross-functional Leadership Teams

Cross-functional leadership, like leadership in general, needs to permeate throughout the various levels of the organization. Cross-functional management occurs as a result of key management people meeting periodically to ensure that key business performance areas that cross functional boundaries are managed effectively.

Some of the key business performance areas can be:

- Quality of products or service
- Quantity of products or service
- Cost of products or service
- Delivery time
- Safety
- Environment

Operational Leadership Teams

The operational leadership teams are usually the point where "the buck stops." They are the ones who manage the resources that produce the products or services which the client or customer uses.

Project Teams

Project teams are those groups (generally cross-functional in makeup) who are designated or take on a special assignment to achieve a specific goal or mandate identified as an opportunity to improve business performance. They usually have a clear mandate with deliverables and a time frame for completion. Project teams are not permanent in nature and usually disband after completion of their assignment.

Natural Work Groups

Natural work groups, on the other hand, are more permanent. They are usually involved in common processes that deliver a product or service to the ultimate customer or to some internal group or groups within the organization. Included in this could be:

- A group of operators in a chemical plant
- Computer analysts
- A training-development group
- A group of supervisors who meet to work on employee development

Technical Support

Technical support people can be either internal or external to the organization. These are the people who provide special expertise in some special performance area of the organization. Generally, they gather and analyze data in certain key areas of business performance and provide feedback to the organization. They also provide coaching and support to those who work in the organization's processes. Some of these technical support areas are:

- Human resource development
- Safety
- Accounting and financial data

- Process technical expertise
- Data collection and analysis
- Maintenance specialties (for example, instrumentation, rotating equipment, inspection, or electrical)

Process Coach

A process coach provides a somewhat different role in an organization. This is someone who is knowledgeable in the change process. There are two components to the role of a process coach. One component is to ensure a discipline in the following of the process, thus allowing the team to focus on the content of the problem. This is a facilitative role and one which a skilled team leader is frequently adept at playing. However, some issues may be sufficiently complex to warrant input to the content of the problem by the team leader. In such cases, identifying a neutral facilitator then becomes important.

The other role of a process coach is to support the ongoing planning process. This is an area in which a third party (a process coach) helps the team leader prepare for team meetings, assess progress and coach the team leader as the project unfolds.

Personal Coach

A personal coach is someone who helps individuals become the best they can be. This should be someone who has good listening skills and will be empathetic, and who has the ability to help individuals identify what may be holding them back. An effective personal coach will help individuals put in place plans and structures that will move them forward. Although this is a role usually intended for the supervisor of the employee, experience has shown that it is very difficult for one individual to be both judge and coach. Organizations might be well served to train employees to be good personal coaches for each other.

Systems

Thinking

Systems Thinking

Understanding Systems

Managing Improvement and Quality Control are about understanding the fundamental principles (the cause-and-effect relationships) that occur within systems. In addition, they are about using such understanding to ensure that all aspects of the system are performing at their optimum.

This section will focus on understanding the attributes of systems. In order to do so, we will have a look at systems from a more generic point of view and try to understand the key elements that must be in place to ensure reliable performance. We will discuss which systems are inherent to an organization and, in particular, to examine the attributes of *Continuous Improvement,* one of the key organizational subsystems.

What is a System?

"A system is a set or arrangement of things so related or connected as to form a unity or organic whole; as, a solar system, irrigation system, and supply system" (*Webster's New Twentieth Century Unabridged Dictionary—second edition*, 1985).

Russell Ackoff (GOAL/QPC conference, 1993) defines a system as consisting of a set of parts (elements).

- Each of which can affect the essential (defining) functional behaviours, or property of the whole.

- The way each affect the whole depends on what, at least, one other part is doing, that is, no part has an independent effect on the whole.

- Every possible subgroup of these parts can affect the essential (defining) functional behaviour or property of the whole, but none can have an independent effect on it.

Objectives   This section on **systems thinking** will:

- Describe the different types of systems and how their purposes are to be understood
- List and describe the eight components of Jerry Nadler's Hopper Model of a system

- Describe the system attributes of a business organization
- Describe the three key subsystems of a business organization
- Describe the system attributes of a continuous improvement system
- Describe the Managing Improvement model for managing continuous improvement
- Use the systems matrix to ensure that a system under development or review is complete

Different Types of Systems

According to Ackoff, (GOAL/QPC conference, 1993) there are three principal types of systems:

Mechanistic

Has no purpose of its own.
Example: A clock or the solar system.

Biological

Has a purpose of its own. Primary purpose is survival and growth.
Example: A living organism such as a cow, a pig, or a human being.

Social

Has a purpose of its own, but also has parts with purposes of their own that are affected by outside forces with purposes of their own.
Example: A business, hospital, a community, or a country.

Understanding a System's Purpose

It is important to note that you can never understand a system's purpose by examining its parts.

Ackoff (GOAL/QPC conference, 1993) states that:

- You can never understand a system by analyzing it;
- Understanding a system always lies outside the system and not inside;
- You need to understand a system in the context of the systems within which it operates.

A Systems Model

Introduction

In trying to understand a system, it is useful to have a framework or model for analysis from which to predict its performance, analyze its underperformance, or install a new system. Gerald Nadler's Hopper model is useful for identifying what needs to be in place in order to implement a new system, or to take corrective action on a management system which is not functioning at its best.

"All models are incomplete, but some are useful," says Nadler. (Nadler, 1990)

Hopper Model Showing the Eight Components of a System

The diagram below can help to understand the various attributes of a system. An explanation of the process flow of the system is also provided.

Fig. 9: The Hopper Model of a Social System (as proposed by Nadler)

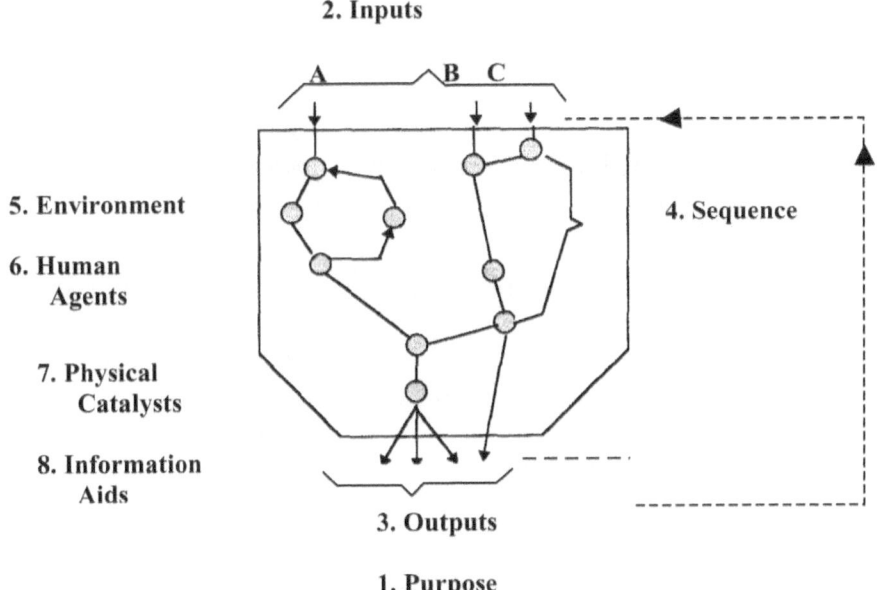

The process flow of the system depicts how inputs (2) are taken in and processed through a set of steps or sequences (4) to generate outputs (3) and thus serve the purpose of the system (1). The system works within an environment (5), which requires human agents (6), physical catalysts (7) and communication systems (information aids) (8) in order to make it function.

According to Nadler, a social system has eight distinct attributes (three external and five internal), which are as follows:

External:

1. Purpose	mission, aim, need, primary concern, focus;
2. Inputs	people, things, information to start the sequence;
3. Outputs	(which achieve purpose) and desired outcomes from sequence.

Internal:

4. Sequence	steps for processing inputs, flow, layout, unit operations;
5. Environment	includes physical and attitudinal, organization and setting;
6. Human Agents	includes skilled personnel, responsibilities and rewards;
7. Physical Catalysts	includes equipment and facilities;
8. Information Aids	includes books and instructions.

Synonymous Terms and Their Meanings

The term *process* is frequently used synonymously with the term *system*. Here, the term *process* is used to denote a set of subsystems or steps that are required to take inputs and turn them into outputs for the overall system being examined.

Example 1   An Irrigation System

External:

    Purpose   Hierarchy of purposes:

        1.   To feed the world

        2.   To feed the local people

        3.   To provide an income for the owner

        4.   To water the vegetation (for example: hay, trees, grass, or grain)

    Inputs

- Vegetation requiring water
- Water
- Irrigation equipment from suppliers

    Outputs

- Distributed water
- Growing vegetation

Internal:

    Sequence

1. Recognize need to turn system on
2. Move sprinkler system to location needing water
3. Turn pump on
4. Adjust sprinkler system
5. Move sprinklers as required
6. Recognize when sufficient water has been distributed
7. Shut off pump

    Environment

- Arid conditions
- Water for irrigation available

- Farmer with sufficient funds and resources to irrigate the land
- Land that requires irrigation
- A need for the product of irrigation

Human Agents

- Individual(s) to operate the irrigation equipment

Physical Catalysts

- Pump
- Irrigation equipment
- Land

Information aids

- Operating instructions for equipment
- Repair instructions for equipment
- Market information
- Weather information

Example 2   The Pumping System (for the irrigation system)

It is important to understand that there are systems within systems (internal systems) as well as systems that are externally connected with other systems. The interplay of systems can be extremely complex.

External:

Purpose   Hierarchy of purposes:
- To provide the water necessary for the irrigation system

Inputs

- Water
- Electricity or gas, depending on the energy source
- Maintenance materials

Outputs

- Pressurized water

Internal:

Sequence

1. Open suction valve
2. Ensure the pump is primed
3. Start pump
4. Check that pressure is sufficient
5. Check that water is flowing
6. Shut down pump when it is finished

Environment

- Air for cooling the pump motor;
- Grounded motor.

Human Agents

- Individual(s) who know how to operate the pump and motor.

Physical Catalysts

- Pump;
- Motor;
- Electric or gas engine.

Information aids

- Operating instructions for pump and motor;
- Repair instructions for equipment;
- Troubleshooting guides;
- Pressure and flow gauges.

Importance of Understanding the Connection between Systems and Subsystems

Systems are seldom independent. They are usually parts of larger systems in which they play a role, and they are affected by other systems both external and internal to themselves. Ecologists have certainly explored the significance of this issue. They have voiced their concerns about the hazards of destroying one ecological system to the detriment of other, seemingly unrelated, ecosystems. This same concept applies to the business organization. We must not only understand the key elements of the system we are concerned with; we must also seek to understand how this system interrelates with other systems internal and external to the organization. This is important to understand so that we don't try to optimize one at the expense of another.

Business Organizations as a System

Definition of an Organization

An organization is any unified, consolidated group of elements; systematized whole; especially, a body of persons organized for some specific purpose, as a club, union, or society.

A business is "the employment; occupation; profession; calling; vocation; means of livelihood; that which occupies the time; attention, and labour of men, for the purpose of profit or improvement; as his business was that of a merchant; the business of a banker"

A business organization is a social system with attributes similar to those of other systems. The following examples are some possible attributes of a business organization:

System Attributes of a Business Organization

External:

Purpose

Hierarchy of purposes:
- To make the world a better place to live in
- To provide quality products for the needs of the marketplace
- To make a profit for the shareholders
- To provide jobs

Inputs

- Requests for quality products and services
- Raw materials
- Maintenance supplies

Outputs

- Quality products and services
- Tax dollars for community services
- In some cases pollutants
- Jobs and wages
- Dividends to the shareholders

Internal:

Sequence

In the case of a business, there are three primary subsystems:

1. Meeting Customer Needs:

The primary system consists of a set of processes that take the customer requests and generate delivered products or services, collects the payments and generates a profit. This system is comprised of sub-processes such as:

a) Market and sell

b) Produce product

c) Deliver product

d) Collect payment and pay the bills

e) Develop new products and services

2. Setting the Standard:

Some of the sub-processes for this system are:

a) Market trend analysis

b) Customer needs assessment

c) Competitor analysis

d) Mission and vision development

e) Establishment of company values

f) Company goal setting

3. Continuous Improvement:

The primary sub-processes for this system are:

    a) Breakthrough

    b) Incremental improvement

    c) Quality control or standardization

Environment

- Market conditions
- Company values
- Geographic location
- Labour availability
- Raw material
- Government regulations
- Public opinion

Human Agents

- Technical people
- Management
- Accounting specialists
- Safety specialists
- Information systems specialists
- Maintenance
- Procurement specialists
- Human resource specialists
- Research and development (R and D) specialists

Physical Catalysts

- Buildings
- Process equipment
- Delivery equipment
- Information systems equipment (i.e., computers)

Information aids

- E-mail
- Bulletin boards
- Planning boards
- Communication meetings
- Company magazines

Continuous Improvement as a System

Introduction

Continuous improvement has always been important to a business organization. Within the last few years it has become increasingly more important. Whereas incremental improvement was sufficient to maintaining a competitive advantage in the past, it has now become imperative (while maintaining the gains that have been made) to achieve breakthrough or discontinuous improvement.

As mentioned in the introduction, Dr. Michael Porter states that competitive advantage is essentially attainable through differentiation. Differentiation is achieved by either inventing a product or service that is not easily duplicated by the competition or improving at a rate faster than the competition. Since inventing a product or service that cannot be easily duplicated is a difficult task, improving at a rate faster than the competition is a more viable strategy.

Continuous Improvement has the same attributes as the previously discussed systems.

Definition of Continuous Improvement

Continuous Improvement is the system that fosters a customer-focused, strategic and organized approach by everyone toward continuous performance improvement. CI has both external and internal attributes.

System Attributes of a Continuous Improvement System

External:

Purpose

The purpose of a Continuous Improvement system is to maintain the long-term viability of an organization through focusing on meeting the needs of its key stakeholders at a rate faster than the competition.

Inputs

- Business direction
- Technology
- Customer needs
- Employee needs
- Societal needs
- Employee ideas for improvement
- Technical innovation

Outputs

- Improved processes
- Control systems

Internal:

Sequence

In the case of continuous improvement, there are three primary processes:

- Breakthrough or discontinuous change
- Incremental change
- Quality control (QC) or standardization (the process of building in control systems to maintain the change until the next change occurs)

Environment

- Market conditions
- Competition
- Company values
- Education of employees
- Management that supports improvement (in principle and by supplying time and resources)
- Government regulations
- Public opinion

Human Agents

- Technical specialists
- Management
- Improvement coaches
- Information systems specialists
- R and D specialists

Physical Catalysts

- Meeting rooms
- Visual aids for group work (flipcharts, overheads, etc.)
- Information systems equipment (computers)
- Data-gathering and experimentation equipment

Information aids

- E-mail, answering machine, facsimiles
- Bulletin boards
- Improvement tracking systems
- Project planning boards
- Return on investment (ROI) calculation procedures
- Control and run charts
- Communication meetings
- Company magazines

The question that now arises is: how does a business organization manage improvement in a systematic and proactive manner? The way to do this is through the use of a Continuous Improvement model.

Managing Improvement—The Basic Continuous Improvement (CI) Model

The model for continuous improvement, as developed by the author, comes from the plan, do, check, act (PDAC) cycle or model originally described by Shewhart and later made more famous by Dr. Deming. The MI process exemplifies this fundamental model.

Fig. 10:   The Managing Improvement Process

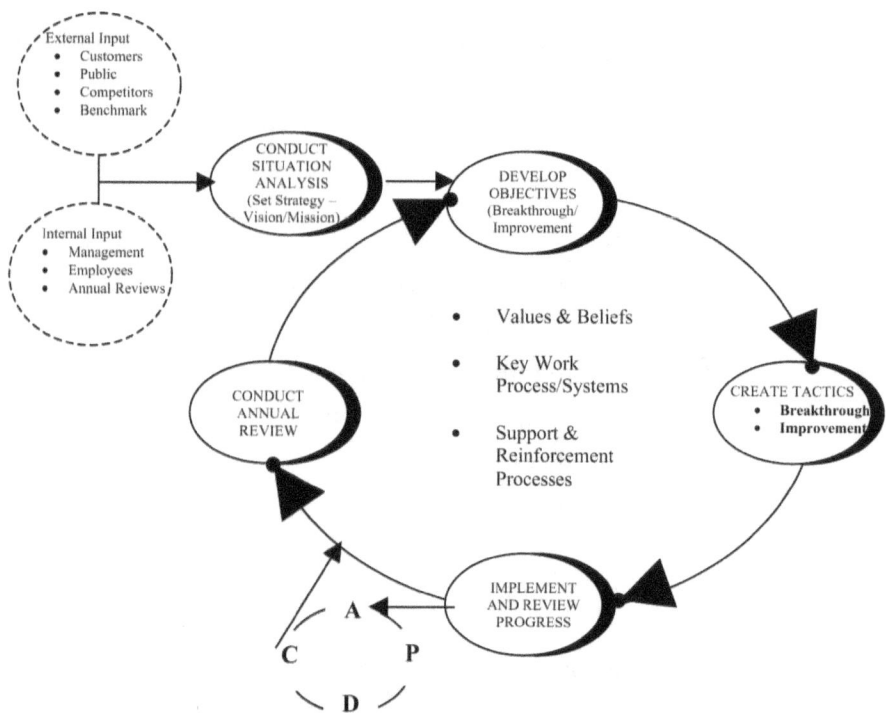

Alignment of Managing Improvement across the Organization

The MI model is multi-dimensional. It is applied at various levels within an organization vertically (up and down the hierarchy) and horizontally (across functions and departments). Interconnections occur at key points, such as at the goal-setting and implementation review stages.

The diagram on the next page shows MI as a linear process on the vertical axis with horizontal interconnections between the various management levels in the organization.

Fig. 11: Describes How Managing Improvement is Aligned throughout a Business Organization

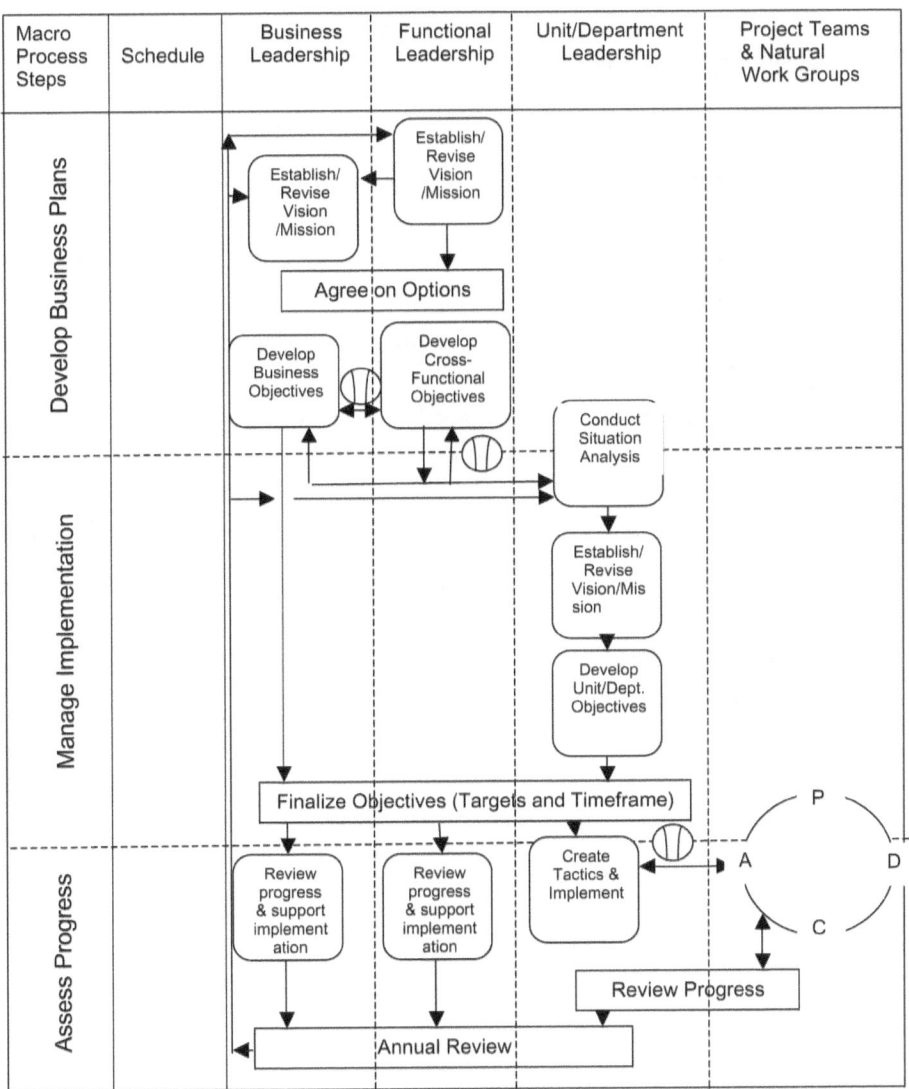

Systems Matrix

The Systems Matrix—What Is It?

The systems matrix is a tool developed by Gerald Nadler (1990) to help in assessing and ensuring that existing and new systems are complete.

What a System Matrix Does

It provides:

- A language for discussing and describing solutions, as well as ideas and recommendations
- Detailed specifications of the fundamental structure that is to exist after installation and implementation
- Information on how a structure or solution will operate or flow over time once it has been activated
- The major activities and events needed to move from presentation and approval of the recommended solution to the time when the structure and its operation are in place
- Documentation of the solution after next (SAN) and the recommendation
- Protection against complacency arising from the assumption that the solution or answer is simple
- Speculation about the future
- A focus on the important elements and dimensions

Table 1: An Example of a Systems Matrix for Assessing Old and Developing New Systems

Dimensions

System Attributes	Fundamental: basic or physical characteristics – what, how, where, or who	Values: Goals, motivating beliefs, global desires, ethics, moral matters	Measures: Performance (criteria, merit and worth factors), objectives (how much, when, rates, performance specifications)	Control: How to evaluate and modify element of system as it operates	Interface: Relation of all dimensions to other systems or elements	Future: Planned changes and research needs for all dimensions
Purpose: mission, aim, need, primary concern, focus						
Inputs: people, things, information to start the sequence						
Outputs desired: (achieves purpose) and desired outcomes from sequence						
Sequence steps for processing inputs, flow, layout, unit operations						
Environment: Includes physical and attitudinal organization and setting						
Human Agents: Includes: skills personnel, responsibilities and rewards						
Physical catalysts: Includes equipment and facilities						
Information aids: Includes books and instructions						

Note:

Models are always incomplete, and the Hopper Model is no exception. Form or structure needs to be added to the elements for completeness.

The number of dimensions in the above matrix is not fixed; some can be divided into two or more attributes.

Qualities of or Definitions of Systems Matrix Terms

Fundamental
: This concerns tangible, overt, observable, physical or basic structural characteristics, including the basic what-who-how-where specifications and quality levels.

Values and Goals
: These are motivating beliefs, human expectations, global desires, ethics, equity and moral concerns that can be ascribed in some form to each element.

Measures
: Translate the values dimension into particular performance factors and operational objectives (how much and when).

Control
: Comprises methods for ensuring that the fundamental, measures and even value specifications are maintained during the operation of the system.

Interface
: Is the relationship of the fundamental, values, measures and control specifications to other internal elements and to external systems.

Future
: Anticipates changes in each specification of the other five dimensions at one or more points of time in the future.

Nine Guidelines for Utilizing the Systems Matrix to Assess an Existing System or Develop a New System:

1. Assume the system matrix is empty when you start a project.
2. Understand that the matrix is an analytical tool (trying to fill in all the rectangles would not be productive).
3. Think elements first, and then expand each element as needed by the dimensions.
4. Transfer any detail activity from the whole system matrix to separate pages if the complexity gets too great.

5. Establish the system matrix as a language of communication in networks of like-minded people.

6. Convert the system matrix into the format used by your specific organization.

7. Find causes and relationships.

8. Provide an integrating and coordinating framework to handle the many available techniques, tools and analysis models.

9. Get people to be mindful of quality and productivity in terms of total systems.

Table 2.   How the System Matrix Can Enhance a Strategic Plan

Strategic Business Unit Plan Format	Elements and Dimensions of System Matrix	Some Possible Other Items to Include
Mission	Purpose Fundamental, values (assumes hierarchy, but not identified) Outputs Interface, future	How to control mission What future missions or purposes How mission relates to other elements
Key environment assumptions	Environment Fundamental, measures, control, interface Outputs Control, interface	Values of environment Future prospects of environment
Key competitor assumptions	Inputs Measures, interface Outputs Measures, control, interface	Specific fundamental inputs Values of competitors Fundamental outputs, how and future
Constraints	(Government regulations could fit in several cells) Purpose Values	Should avoid, but include only external factors not worth trying to change
Objectives	Purpose Measures, future	Relate to purpose values

Goals	Purpose Measures, future Output Measures, future	Relate to values dimension
Strategy	Sequence Fundamental, values Measures, control	Fundamental and future dimensions of outputs
Programs	Purpose Interface Output Interface	Future outputs Interface purpose and outputs
Resources	(Very broad; could include some inputs, human agents, physical catalysts and infor- mation aids)	(See items in parentheses left)
Strategic Business Unit Plan Format	Elements and Dimensions of System Matrix	Some Possible Other Items to Include
Contingencies "What it?"	Inputs, outputs, sequence, environment, human agents Fundamental, control	Triggering mechanism
Financial Forecast	Purpose Measures, future Outputs Output, sequence	
Strategic Business Unit Plan Format	Elements and Dimensions of System Matrix	Some possible other items to include

Other possible factors suggested by system matrix to include in strategic plan format:

Human agents' (workers/managers) development   Technological progression
Compensation schemes   Market prospects
Information systems/flow for decision making   Physical environment changes
Management personnel backup   New material to serve as inputs
Physical facilities projection   Management style

Note: Information for the systems matrix is taken from a presentation made by Gerald Nadler.

Managing

Improvement

(The Process)

The Managing Improvement Process

Objective

If diligently applied, Managing Improvement will help everyone in the organization improve their skills at developing realistic goals and objectives and their ability to achieve them. The organizational performance measures for this process are:

- Objective's target versus actual goal achieved in per cent
- Target time frame for achieving objectives versus actual time frame in per cent
- Efficiency of setting and achieving objectives (man-hours and dollars to develop and achieve objectives)

Managing Improvement helps managers improve their ability to:

- Conduct a situational analysis
- Develop performance measures
- Develop and align breakthrough and improvement objectives functionally and cross-functionally
- Through root-cause analysis, identify tactics for the achievement of the objectives
- Identify support structures, knowledge and skill requirements for implementers, and leadership actions necessary to ensure implementation of the tactics
- Conduct ongoing progress reviews
- Conduct a formal annual review assessment with action plans for improving the performance of the results and of management's ability to conduct the Managing Improvement process

If you always do what you've always done, then you'll always get what you've always gotten.

—Anonymous

Overview

In the previous sections, you learned about key elements which must be in place in order for systems in general, and a continuous improvement system in particular, to function effectively. These key elements include: purpose, inputs, outputs, values and beliefs, key processes, organizational structures and communication systems.

This section describes purposes, inputs, actions and outputs used by the organization's management team during each phase of the MI) process.

Synonymous terms used in place of MI

Some of the most frequent terms that are used in place of Managing Improvement are management by policy, Hoshin planning, Hoshin Kanri, policy deployment, or management by planning.

Definitions of Hoshin Kanri

> Perhaps the most accurate term for Hoshin Kanri would be target-means deployment, but the dryness of that fails to capture the power of this method. Hoshin means shining metal, compass, or pointing, the direction; Kanri means management or control. Hoshin is often translated as policy, but it refers to something more far reaching, like the vision, purpose, or long-term direction of the company, Hoshin Kanri is a method devised to capture and concretize strategic goals as well as flashes of insight about the future and develop the means to bring these into reality.

> With Hoshin Kanri, insight and vision are not lost; plans are not rolled up on the charts of week-long planning meetings and forgotten until next year. The daily crush of events and quarterly bottom-line pressures do not take precedence over strategic plans, rather, these short-term activities are determined and managed by the plans themselves. (Akao 1991)

A shorter definition:

> Hoshin Kanri can be defined as all organizational activities for systematically accomplishing the long and mid-term goals as well as yearly business targets, which are established as the means to achieve business goals. In many cases, it is used for yearly targets. (Akao 1991

Definition of Managing Improvement

Managing Improvement carries all the same definitions of Hoshin Kanri with the inclusion of managing of breakthrough improvement as well as incremental improvement and quality control. Some companies refer to the breakthrough improvement as Hoshin, and to incremental improvement and quality control as daily management or managing business fundamentals. Both these aspects are incorporated into Managing Improvement.

Managing Improvement is not the reengineering process, nor is it the team continuous improvement process. It is the process which ensures that breakthrough improvement, continuous improvement and standardization are focused on the organization's vision, and that management is continually learning how to do this better.

Managing Improvement is the overriding, proactive management coordination and learning process by which the organization's vision is worked towards and through which competitive advantage is achieved.

In short, Managing Improvement is "the learning process that management uses for achieving the organization's vision through involving everyone in a strategic and organized approach towards continuous performance improvement"

Explanation of Objectives and Goals

Long-term objective is a term used throughout this section of the manual. It refers to the combination of business and cross-functional objectives that are deployed to the Department/Operational Management Team (D/OMT). They are usually in a five- to seven-year time frame.

Mid-term objectives are usually the breakthrough objectives that the D/OMT sets for itself. They are typically two to three years in duration.

Annual goals are improvement goals set according to the department's key performance measures. They are determined by summing the incremental improvements that are going on within a department. These goals, as the name implies, are typically set yearly.

Description of Management Teams

The D/OMT is the management group which has the prime responsibility for managing and optimizing the resources used for providing the product or service to the client or customer.

Note: Although the above is the main target group for this book, the managing improvement model is essentially the same at all levels.

Business Management Team (BMT) refers to the leadership group which is responsible for developing high-quality, value-maximizing, customer-focused, realistic objectives. In essence, this means maximizing product or service return on investment (ROI). The BMT ensures that all departments are aligned with overall objectives and strategies, and provides support during implementation. The BMT business objectives are a key input to the D/OMT using the Managing Improvement process. The BMT is a higher level of management than the D/OMT and is usually accountable for a number of different businesses; the D/OMT is only one of them. In many cases, the MI process will be applied to stand-alone businesses that have all functions of the business in one location—functions such as marketing, sales, information systems, procurement, etc. If this is the case, then the BMT is just the local management or D/OMT.

Cross-functional Management Teams (CFMT) are made up of groups of managers from the BMT whose departments have a primary effect or input into the crucial business performance areas. This could include (but is not limited to) such performance areas as quality, quantity, cost (productivity), delivery, safety and environmental performance. Often, these various teams are comprised of some of the same people who are part of the BMTs. In addition, these teams usually have a resource person from the technical aspect of the performance area in question. For example, the safety cross-functional team would have an individual from the safety function as part of the team.

Cross-functional management is of most concern where an organization has multiple businesses, or where a single business has multiple departments or operational teams. In the case of multiple businesses, business leaders frequently form a corporate team to manage the company's overall interests. These individuals also sit on cross-functional teams in order to ensure that the key performance areas are managed across the businesses. In small, single-business companies, cross-functional issues can be managed by the business leadership team as a single body.

The diagram below depicts how this model of cross-functional management might be structured.

Fig. 12: An Example of How Management Team Membership Might be
Distributed Cross-functionally

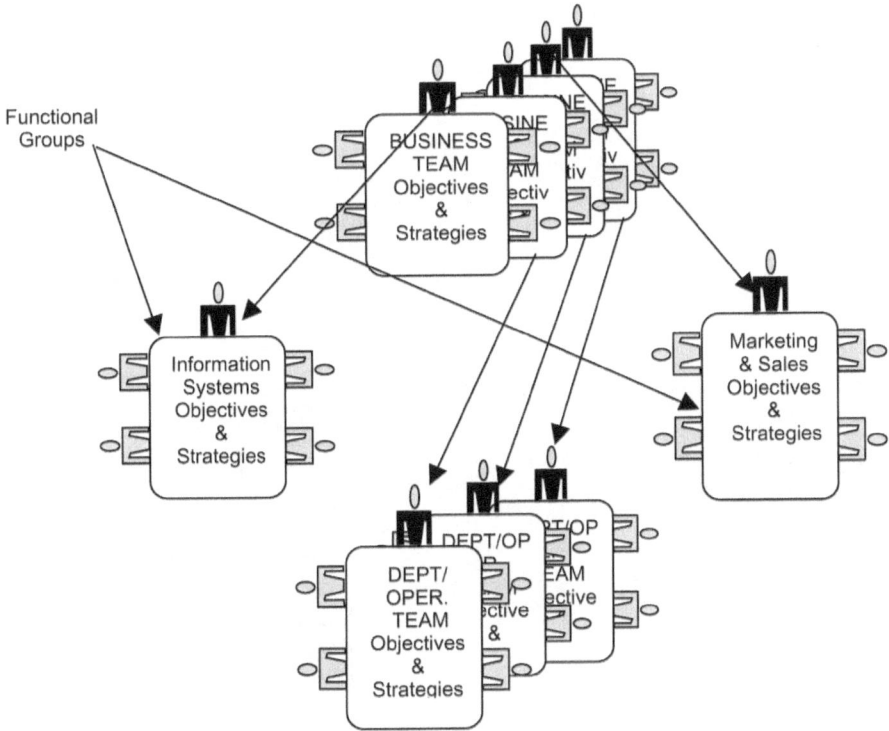

Fig. 13: An Example of How Managing Improvement Might Be Connected Vertically and Cross-functionally

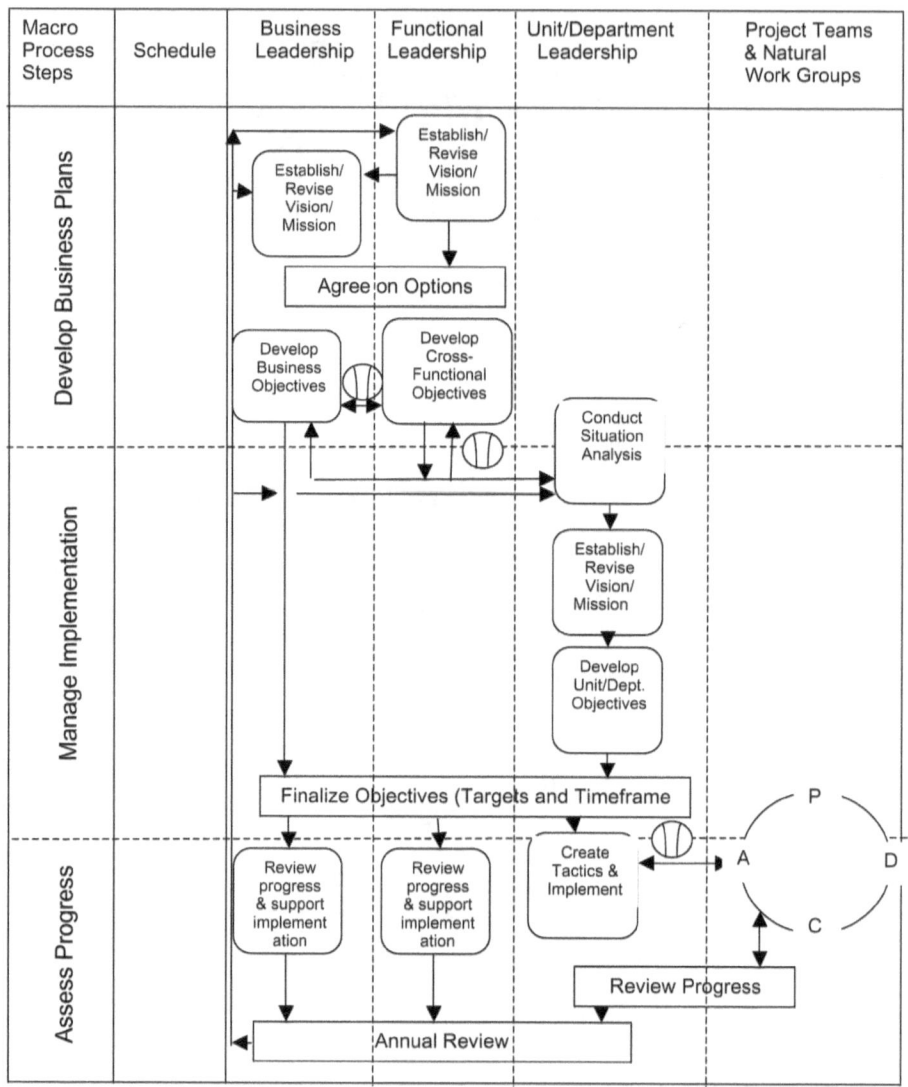

Introduction

The Managing Improvement process consists of five phases. Each phase has a systematic series of steps and key actions that convert inputs to outputs.

The first phase, conducting a Situation Analysis for a department, involves an internal assessment of what is required to support business and cross-functional management objectives, as well as how to address local issues.

Note: The appendix includes an example of a Situation Analysis at the business-team level. It identifies what needs to be done and how.

Note: Many of the examples used throughout this section have been based on a large, multi-level and perhaps multi-national company that has similar businesses spread throughout the country and perhaps internationally. It may be that some of the managers who wish to use this process have only one business or operating plant which produces at only one location. This is perfectly acceptable; just use the material as it is appropriate to your level of operation.

Phase One: Conduct Situation Analysis

Fig. 14:   Managing Improvement Process with Conduct Situation Analysis Highlighted

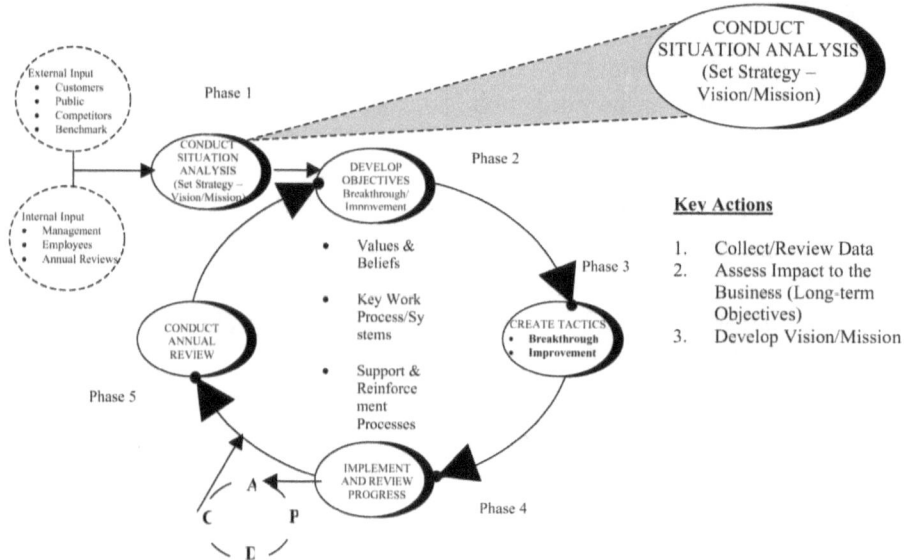

Note: If you are a single-location business or a department or function within a business, then key action two becomes: "Determine Reasons for Improvement."

Note: Setting strategy and mission and/or vision are more significant issues at the business and corporate level of a company. However, it is still important, even at the department or operational level, to establish a mission/vision along with performance measures. Also, note that the key action statement "Develop Vision/Mission" is included as the final action of the Situation Analysis phase. The review and revision of the vision/mission will occur in subsequent annual reviews as part of the ongoing MI process.

Purpose of Conducting a Situation Analysis

For a department, conducting a Situation Analysis involves both root-cause analysis, relating to long-term objectives and identification and analysis of other local issues (particularly those which impact business objectives). It is done for the following reasons:

- To assess previous year's results and local customer issues
- To evaluate where, and to what degree, the D/OMT can impact long-term objectives
- To establish the D/OMT mission and/or vision

Key Action One: Identify Issues

Introduction

In key action one, "Identify Issues," the D/OMT collects data related to long-term objectives and identification of local critical issues. Data collection for the former is quite straightforward, as business priorities are deployed through catch-ball between the BMT and CFMTs (cross-functional management teams). Local issues may require more effort to identify because they stem from several sources.

Inputs

The following list identifies inputs required for this phase.

- Long-term objectives
  - BMT mission and vision and long-term objectives
  - Cross-functional teams' vision and mission and long-term objectives
- Local issues
  - Local customer and/or partner concerns
  - Local regulatory and public issues
  - Employee input (volunteers in the case of not-for-profit organizations)
  - Annual review results
  - Last year's department performance
  - Local competitor assessment
  - Benchmark data

Tools and References

- Cause-and-effect analysis

  (for example, fishbone diagram, brainstorming, process analysis)
- Business quality assessment tools (Malcolm Baldridge Award criteria, Canadian National Quality Institute quality criteria, Deming Award criteria and others)
- System assessment tools (systems matrix, A-B-C analysis, causal loop diagrams, employee surveys)
- Customer or partner surveys (local)

- Benchmarking
- D/OMT objectives table (an example of identified issues is shown below)

Table 3:   D/OMT Objectives

Business		Manager	Date		
Sources of Issues	Current Situation/ Reasons for Improvement	D/OMT Objectives	B/I	Owner	
BMT Business 1. Competitive pressure on costs 2. Customer complaints about product quality **CFMTs** 1. Pressure from work-men's compensation on safety 2. Customer concerns about timely delivery of product 3. Marketing has found new markets for products **Local Issues** 1. Public complaints about air emissions					

Legend: B/I means breakthrough or improvement.

Key Action Two: Assess Impact

Introduction

Potential resolution to local issues and impact on long-term objectives are the focus of key action two. The D/OMT identifies strategic areas for improvement. Response to the questions provided below helps the D/OMT to identify potential contributions to the achievement of the BMT and CFMT long-term objectives.

- What issues impact the business objectives?
- Are there some key issues that prevent achievement of business objectives?
- What do we need to do or have in place?
- What resources are required?

Note: D/OMT team members are often assigned to collect data and champion issues.

Tools and References

- Seven management tools
- Seven QC Tools

An example of a stratification of Pareto analysis (cause and effect) is shown below.

Fig. 15: An Example of a Pareto Analysis for Objectives

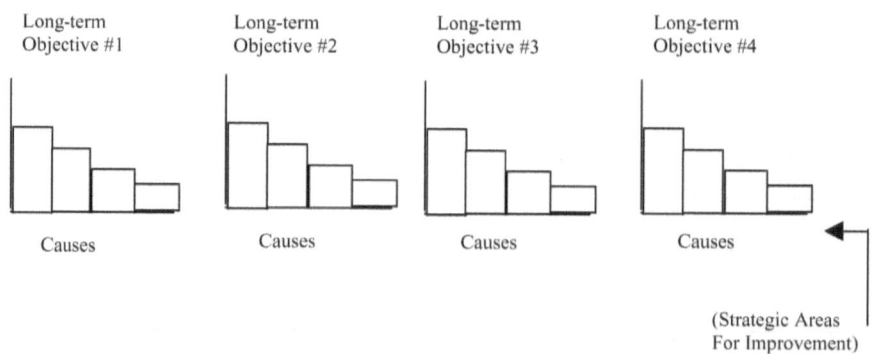

Key Action Three: Develop the Vision/Mission

Introduction

As a result of the previous key actions, the D/OMT is prepared to develop its mission. Long-term objectives with targets serve as the basis for developing mission elements, while strategic areas for improvement can be used to develop the department's intermediate objectives and key performance measures (KPMs).

Note: Although both a vision and a mission can be appropriate at this key-action level, in practice, as MI is moved down the organization to the D/OMT, it becomes more of a mission-building exercise.

Note: "Strategic intent" and "competitive standard" are terms sometimes used by the BMT, essentially describing the business vision. For the D/OMT, strategic intent is defined by its mission statement and key performance areas. Competitive standard is defined as key performance measures (KPMs), which include targets or goals.

Tools and References
*   Mission tree

Outputs

Expected Outputs

Two major outputs result from conducting a Situation Analysis. The first is a department's objective development table. This analysis of the department's current situation or reasons for improvement with respect to business needs and local issues is consolidated in the format shown below. The second output is the mission tree.

Table 4:   Department Objective Development with Reasons for Improvement Identified

Business		Manager	Date	
Sources of Issues	Current Situation/ Reasons for Improvement	D/OMT Objectives	B/I	Owner
BMT Business 1. Competitive pressure on costs 2. Customer complaints about product quality	- Projected data indicates 5% loss in sales over next 5 years. - Competitor analysis indicates customer opinion of key product quality parameters is equal to and in some cases slightly higher for our competitors.			

CFMTs				
1. Pressure from workmen's compensation on safety	- Safety statistics have not shown any improvement over the last two years.			
2. Customer concerns about timely delivery of product	- Complaints about late deliveries have risen 20% in last two years.			
3. Marketing has found new markets for products	- There is an anticipated 20% increase in consumption in our products in Asia within the next 10 years.			
Local Issues				
1. Public complaints about air emissions	- There is a significant danger that the government will impose significant restrictive legislation on our operation.			

Here is an example of a D/OMT mission tree with identified accountabilities for the key performance areas and measures:

Fig. 16: Business Vision/Mission Tree and Key Performance Charts

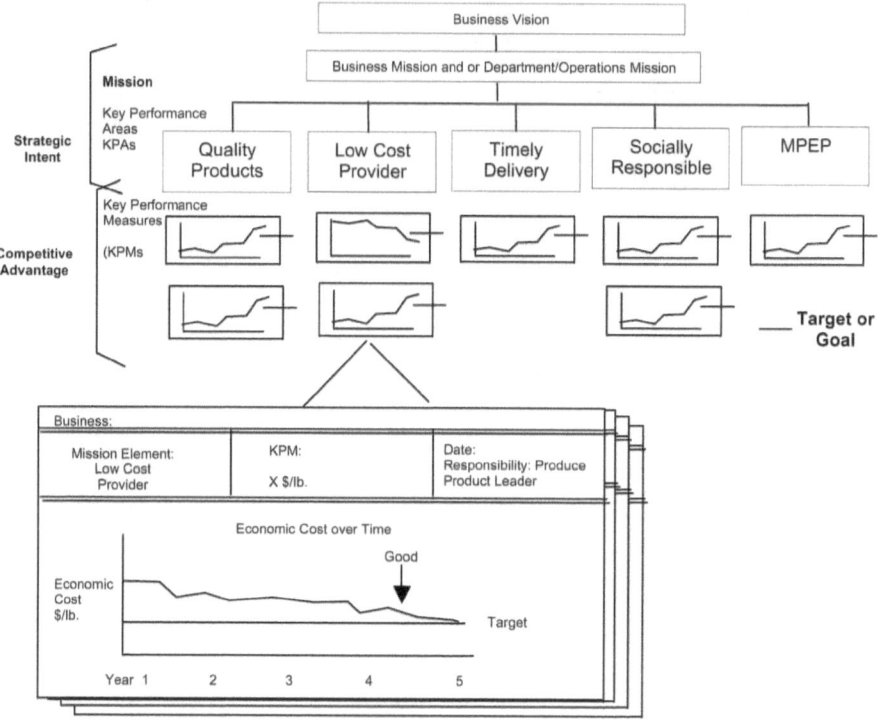

Note: For a stand-alone business, the business management team and operations management team will be one and the same.

Potential Pitfalls

The following list identifies some pitfalls and traps to be aware of and avoid during Situation Analysis.

- Failure to understand the expectations of the business
- Failure to assess local issues adequately—customer, competitor, regulatory and employee concerns
- Failure to benchmark best in class
- Failure to set up clear department performance measures with clearly identified accountabilities

Phase Two: Develop Objectives

Introduction

In phase two, the D/OMT develops objectives and strategies required to achieve long-term targets.

Fig. 17: Managing Improvement Process with Develop Objectives Highlighted

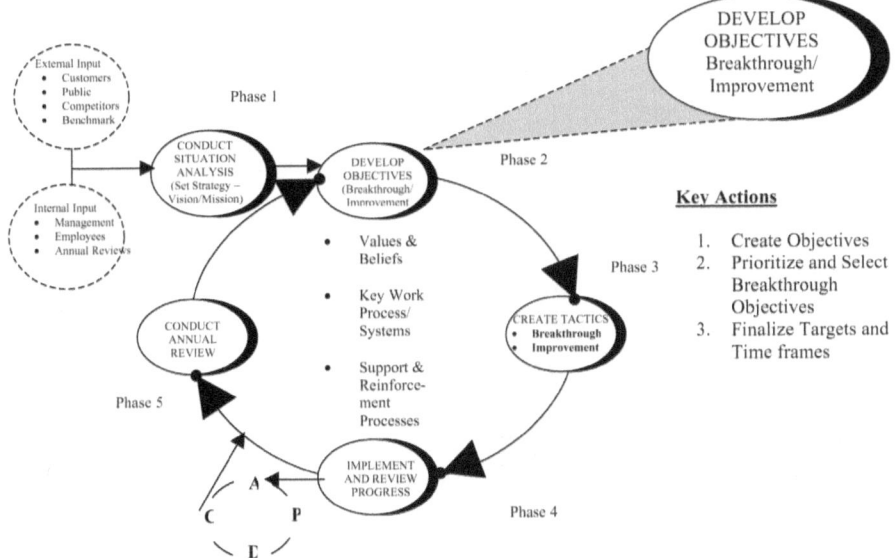

Purpose

The purpose of this phase of MI is to use data to transform both local issues and the business vision into D/OMT objectives—with a major focus on breakthrough. To ensure organizational alignment, the D/OMT finalizes breakthrough objectives and targets through catchball with the BMT and CFMTs.

Note: Improvement objectives are only tentatively identified here. They are confirmed in the next phase, called "Create Plans."

Definition of terms used in phase two

Breakthrough

A breakthrough:

- Results in a major change to one or more processes that impact a key performance measure
- Is cross-functional in nature
- Demands high resource commitments
- At the D/OMT level, requires one to three years to achieve (at the BMT level, it requires up to five to seven years to achieve). These time frames are not set in stone, and for stand-alone businesses they can very well take up to seven years.

Improvement

Improvement focuses on incremental improvement to key work processes. It may be functional or cross-functional in nature. Improvement targets, usually set for one-year periods, are developed as a result of summing up the goals and strategies from natural work group activities.

Inputs for Developing Objectives

The following inputs are required for this phase.
- Long-term business objectives and strategies come from phase one
  - Business objectives
  - CFMTs objectives
- D/OMT mission tree and KPM charts (phase one)
- D/OMT objectives table (phase two)

Key Action One: Create Objectives

Introduction

In this key action, the D/OMT does the following:

- Formulates preliminary D/OMT objectives based on strategic areas of improvement (see objectives table, phase one)
- Analyzes objectives for impact on elements and critical issues
- Assesses potential conflicts that require resolution (for example, contingency planning)
- Creates additional objectives to address any deficiencies

Note: Generally, these objectives are a reflection of the vision/mission key performance measures.

Tools and References
- Mission tree and KPM charts (for reference, see phase one)
- Department objectives table (an example is shown below)

Table 5:   BMT and CFMT Objectives with Tentative Objectives Established

Business			Manager		Date
Sources of Issues	Current Situation/ Reasons for Improvement		D/OMT Objectives	B/I	Owner
BMT Business 1. Competitive pressure on costs 2. Customer complaints about product quality **CFMTs** 1. Pressure from workmen's compensation on safety 2. Customer concerns about timely delivery of product	- Projected data indicates 5% loss in sales over next 5 years. - Competitor analysis indicates customer opinion of key product quality parameters is equal to and in some cases slightly higher for our competitors. - Safety statistics have not shown any improvement over the last two years. - Complaints about late deliveries have risen 20% in last two years.		1.0 Reduce cost to produce by 10% within 5 years 2.0 Achieve statistical quality control within 2 years (eliminate special causes) 3.0 Reduce safety incidents by 20% within 5 years. 4.0 Meet 99% of on-time deliveries within 3 years		

3.	Marketing has found new markets for products	-	There is an anticipated 80% increase in consumption in our products in Asia within the next 10 years.	5.0 Increase production by 20% within 5 years.		
Local Issues						
4.	Public complaints about air emissions	-	There is a significant danger that the government will impose significant restrictive legislation on our operation.	6.0 Reduce emissions by 50% within 2 years		

Note: These objectives are only tentative. They need to be firmed up through catchball with those who have to establish and implement the plans.

Key Action Two: Prioritize and Select Breakthrough Objectives

Introduction

This key action involves evaluating objectives, sorting them for breakthrough or improvement and adding targets and time frames for completion. The following activities occur here:

- Prioritize preliminary objectives (based on greatest impact and achievability)
- Select the most important objectives for breakthrough
  - Set initial targets and time frames; assign accountabilities for breakthrough objectives
  - Develop tactics—first level stratification—for achievement of objectives (based on reasons for improvement)
  - Estimate capital and resource requirements
- Recommendation: Limit breakthrough objectives to one (two at a maximum), as they require extensive effort and typically can take up to five years to accomplish.
- Note: Non-breakthrough objectives are to be considered as potential improvement issues. They are used as input in phase three.

Tools and References

- Management tools
- Y Matrix: a tool for prioritizing the objectives using:
  - Vision key performance areas as the criteria
  - Issues that are barriers to the achievement of the vision key performance areas.

Fig. 18:   Y Matrix

Example of a Y Matrix sheet:

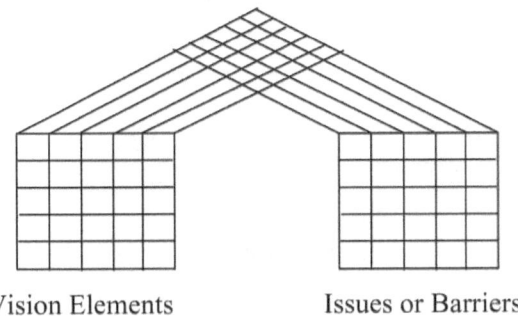

Vision Elements   Issues or Barriers

- Objectives:
- Strategy tree: A tool for working backwards from the desired end point to specific plans that have to be worked on to achieve the objective, strategies and tactics.
- Planning board: A tool for capturing all the relevant information about a particular breakthrough objective (including what it is, the key strategies, tactics and plans, who is accountable and the performance measure)
- Department breakthrough objectives (tentative targets)

An Example of an Objective Planning Table

Table 6:   Department Breakthrough Objectives Example

Business		Manager		Date
Sources of Issues	Current Situation/ Reasons for Improvement	D/OMT Objectives	B/I	Owner
BMT Business				
1. Competitive pressure on costs	- Projected data indicates 5% loss in sales over next 5 years.	1. Reduce cost to produce by 10% within 5 years	B	
2. Customer complaints about product quality	- Competitor analysis indicates customer opinion of key product quality parameters is equal to and in some cases slightly higher for our competitors.	2. Achieve statistical quality control within 2 years (eliminate special causes)	I	
CFMTs				
1. Pressure from workmen's compensation on safety	- Safety statistics have not shown any improvement over the last two years.	3. Reduce safety incidents by 20% within 5 years.	B	
2. Customer concerns about timely delivery of product	- Complaints about late deliveries have risen 20% in last two years.	4. Meet 99% of on-time deliveries within 3 years	I	
3. Marketing has found new markets for products	- There is an anticipated 80% increase in consumption in our products in Asia within the next 10 years.	5. Increase production by 20% within 5 years.	B	

Local Issues			
1. Public complaints about air emissions	- There is a significant danger that the government will impose significant restrictive legislation on our operation.	6. Reduce emissions by 50% within 2 years	I

An Example of a Strategy Tree

Fig. 19: Strategy Tree

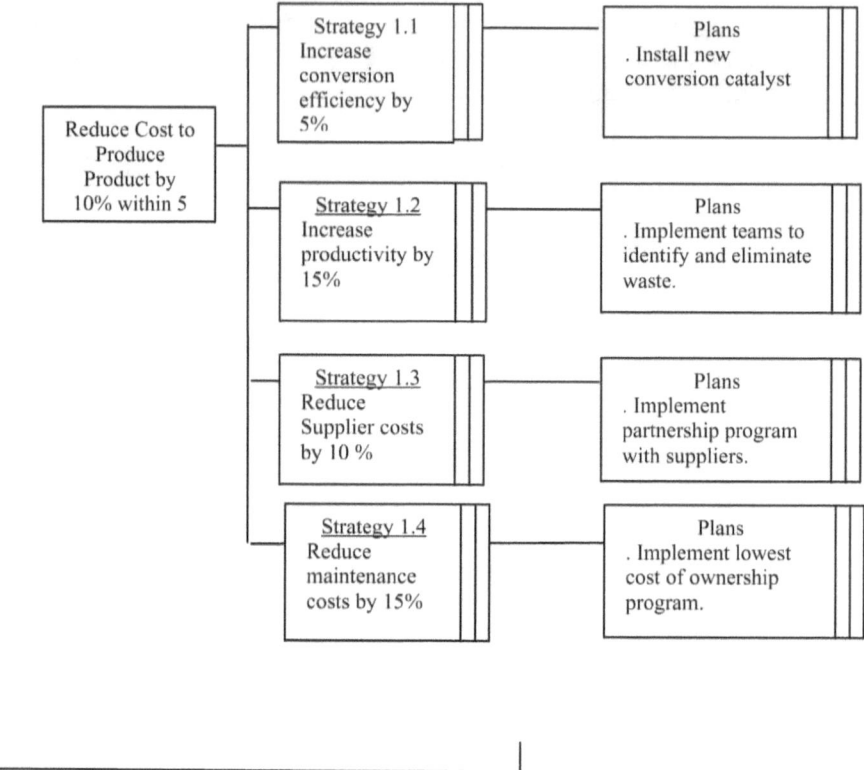

An Example of a Planning Board Sheet

Fig. 20: Planning Board

Objective: Reduce Cost to Produce Product by 10% within 5 yrs.		Target					Mission KPM Chart (w/projected progress)
Formula: Sum of all costs - Marketing							
Coordinator: Produce Product Process Owner							
Strategy	Owner	PM	Schedule Yr. 1 2 3 4 5				
1. Increase conversion efficiency by 5%		Efficiency	------------------				
2. Increase productivity by 15%		Productivity	------------------------------				
3. Reduce Supplier costs by 10 %		Supply costs	-----------------------------------				
4. Reduce maintenance costs by 15%		Maintenance costs	------------------				

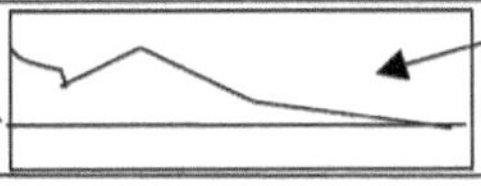

Legend: PM = performance measure

An Example of a Head Count/Capital Matrix

Fig. 21:   Head Count/Capital Matrix

D/OMT Objectives	Reduce Cost to produce by 10%	Reduce safety incidents by 20%	Increase Production by 20 %
Objective #1 Strategies			
1. Increase conversion efficiency by 5%	1 $5.0M		
2. Increase productivity by 15%	0 $2.0M		
3. Reduce Supplier costs by 10 %	0 $0.0		
4. Reduce maintenance costs by 15%	1 $3.0M		
Subtotal	2 $10.0M		
Objective #2 Strategies			

Subtotal			
Objective #3 Strategies			

Subtotal			
Grand Total			

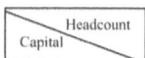
Headcount / Capital

Key Action Three: Finalize Targets

Introduction

In key action three, "Finalize Targets," the D/OMT finalizes breakthrough objectives through catchball discussions with the BMT and CFMTs to attain consensus on an alignment of objectives, targets and time frames.

Tools/References

- Catchball

D/OMT   BMT CFMTs

Expected Outputs

The following outputs are the result of completing this phase.

Fig. 22:   Example of a Modified D/OMT Mission Sheet

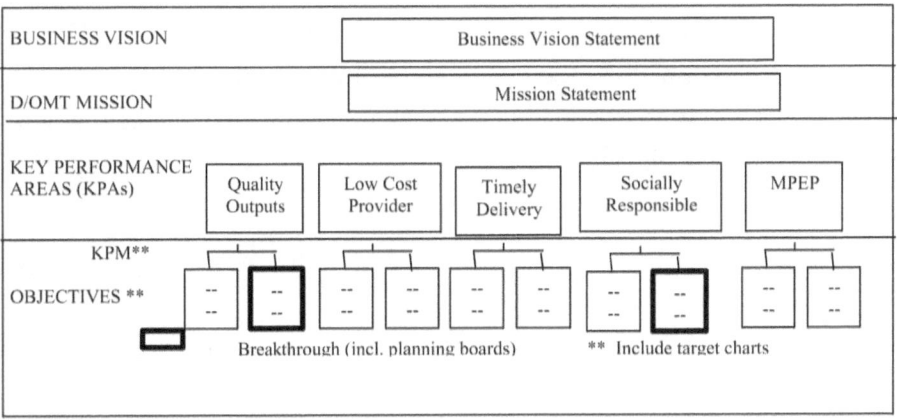

Legend: MPEP = motivated, productive, empowered employees

Fig. 23:   An Example of a Completed D/MOT Breakthrough Planning Board Sheet

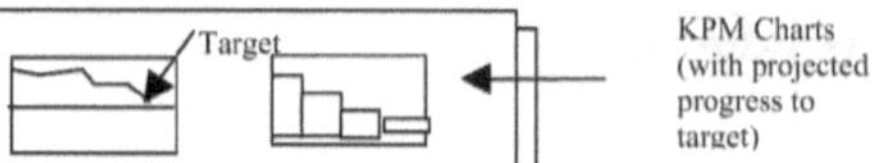

Objective: Reduce Cost to Produce Product by 12% within 5 yrs. Formula: Sum of all costs - Marketing					Target				KPM Charts (with projected progress to target)

Coordinator: Produce Product Process Owner								
Strategy	Owner	PM	Schedule Yr. 1 2 3 4 5					
1. Increase conversion efficiency by 5%		Efficiency		-------------------				
2. Increase productivity by 10%		Productivity		---------------------------				
3. Reduce Supplier costs by 15 %		Supply costs		--------------------------				
4. Reduce maintenance costs by 17%		Maintenance costs		-----------------				

Potential Pitfalls

Be aware of, and try to avoid, potential pitfalls and traps during this phase of MI such as:

- Selection of too many key objectives for available resources
- Failure to establish meaningful targets and time frames
- Not adequately conducting catchball up and down the organization, as well as cross-functionally

Phase Three: Create Tactics

Introduction

This phase of MI involves creating plans for *two concurrent components*—breakthrough and incremental improvement.

Fig. 24:   Managing Improvement Process with Create Tactics Highlighted

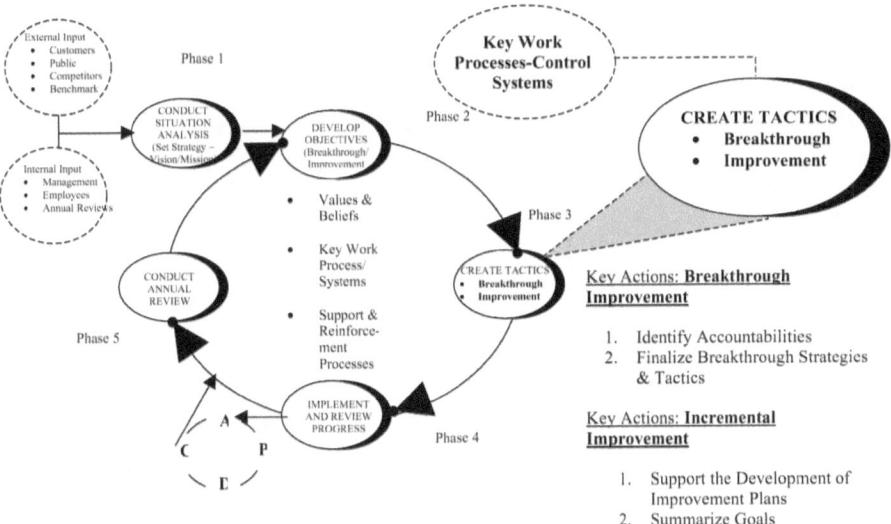

Purpose

The purposes of this phase are to create and communicate sufficient tactics to achieve breakthrough objectives and maintain and improve important operational performance measures.

The breakthrough improvement component ensures alignment of strategies and tactics with targets for D/OMT breakthrough objectives. It also aligns personnel and resources involved with implementing tactics and establishes methods to monitor progress towards achievement of breakthrough objectives.

The incremental improvement component is less formal in nature. It involves finalizing improvement objectives and targets by summing up improvement goals from natural work groups and project teams. This ensures that key operational performance measures are maintained and, where appropriate, incrementally improved.

Breakthrough Improvement

Introduction

The breakthrough improvement component of "Create Tactics" provides a more formal process by which tactics and plans are developed to achieve breakthrough objectives. These tactics are a continuation of the strategies identified in the previous phase.

Definitions of Terms Used in This Phase

Table 7:   Definitions of Terms

Objectives	A desired end point, destination, or goal. It should contain measures with a target and time frame for completion.
Strategies	High-level strategic areas of focus which need to be achieved in order to attain the objective.
Tactics	Lower-level strategic areas of focus which need to be achieved in order to achieve the strategies.
Plans	Sequences of actions which need to occur in order to accomplish the tactics.

In essence, objectives, strategies and tactics are the *whats* that need to be achieved. The plans are the *hows*, or specific actions that need to occur so that the *whats* can be achieved.

Inputs

D/OMT breakthrough objectives (that is, breakthrough planning boards) and key operational work processes (for example, control systems) are the primary inputs required for this part of phase three.

Breakthrough Improvement
Key Action One: Identify Accountabilities

Introduction:

This key action requires the D/OMT to identify who needs to be accountable for achieving each strategy and tactic necessary to achieve the breakthrough objective(s). Project team development and goals or targets for natural work groups will begin to occur in this phase.

In order to determine accountabilities, it is important to identify and select key work processes that impact breakthrough objectives. If the key work processes are not known, or control systems are not in place for them, then control systems need to be part of the project team's mandate to develop.

Tools and References

- Managing daily work: control systems

An example of how the organization's process-control systems become the basis for deciding on accountabilities.

Fig. 25: Connection Between Control Systems and Identifying Accountabilities

Control Systems

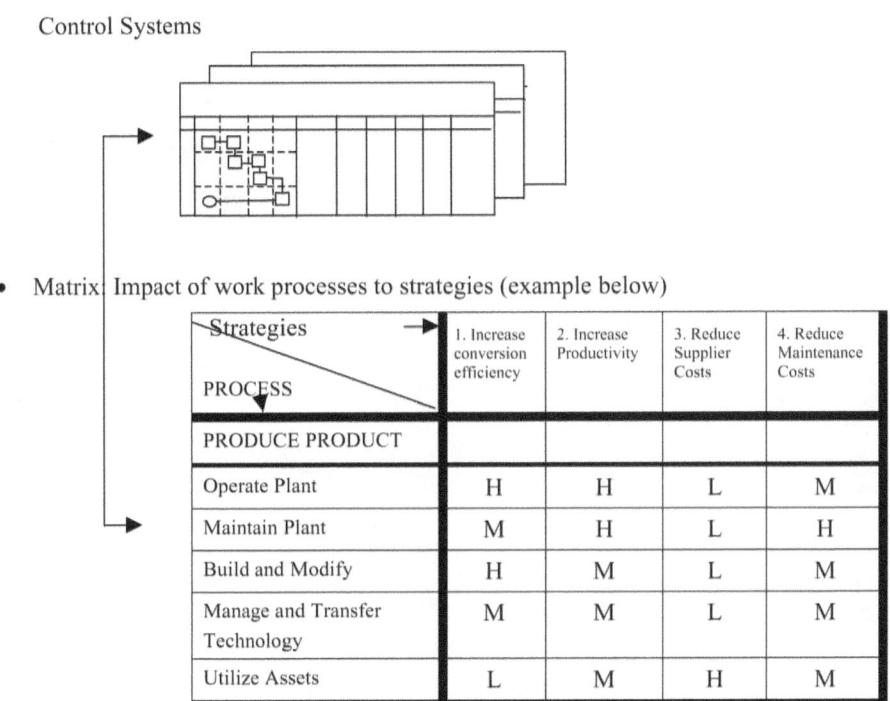

- Matrix Impact of work processes to strategies (example below)

Strategies / PROCESS	1. Increase conversion efficiency	2. Increase Productivity	3. Reduce Supplier Costs	4. Reduce Maintenance Costs
PRODUCE PRODUCT				
Operate Plant	H	H	L	M
Maintain Plant	M	H	L	H
Build and Modify	H	M	L	M
Manage and Transfer Technology	M	M	L	M
Utilize Assets	L	M	H	M

Legend : H – High, M – Medium, L - Low

Table 8:   Department   Breakthrough   Objectives   with
        Accountabilities Identified

Business		Manager	Date	
Sources of Issues	Current Situation/ Reasons for Improvement	D/OMT Objectives	B/I	Owner

BMT Business					
3. Competitive pressure on costs	-	Projected data indicates 5% loss in sales over next 5 years.	4. Reduce cost to produce by 10% within 5 years	B	Produce Product Process Owner
4. Customer complaints about product quality	-	Competitor analysis indicates customer opinion of key product quality parameters is equal to and in some cases slightly higher for our competitors.	5. Achieve statistical quality control within 2 years (eliminate special causes)	I	Produce Product Process Owner
CFMTs					
4. Pressure from workmen's compensation on safety	-	Safety statistics have not shown any improvement over the last two years.	6. Reduce safety incidents by 20% within 5 years.	B	Produce Product Process Owner
5. Customer concerns about timely delivery of product	-	Complaints about late deliveries have risen 20% in last two years.	4. Meet 99% of on-time deliveries within 3 years	I	Integrated Supply Chain Process Owner
6. Marketing has found new markets for products	-	There is an anticipated 80% increase in consumption in our products in Asia within the next 10 years.	5. Increase production by 20% within 5 years.	B	Market/ Sell Process Owner
Local Issues					
2. Public complaints about air emissions	-	There is a significant danger that the government will impose significant restrictive legislation on our operation.	7. Reduce emissions by 50% within 2 years	I	Produce Product Process Owner

Fig. 26:   Planning Board with Accountabilities Finalized

			Target					
Objective: Reduce Cost to Produce Product by 10% within 5 yrs.								
Formula: Sum of all costs - Marketing								
Coordinator: Produce Product Process Owner								
Strategy	Owner	PM	Schedule Yr. 1 2 3 4 5					
1. Increase conversion efficiency by 5%	Build and modify owner	Efficiency	--------------------					
2. Increase productivity by 15%	Produce product owner	Productivity	-------------------------					
3. Reduce Supplier costs by 10%	Utilize Assets owner	Supply costs	----------------------------					
4. Reduce maintenance costs by 15%	Maintain plant owner	Maintenance costs	------------------					

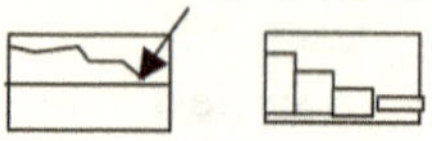

KPM Charts (with projected progress to target)

Breakthrough Improvement
Key Action Two: Finalize Breakthrough Strategies and Tactics

This key action finalizes performance measures and identifies accountabilities for each strategy, tactic or project based on key D/OMT work processes.

It is usually not the D/OMT itself that develop the tactics and plans. Instead, they perform the role of the sponsor or leader of other individuals, project teams, or natural work groups who go out and develop the actual tactics and plans necessary for achieving the D/OMT's objectives and strategies.

The D/OMT's job is to:

- Record breakthrough tactics onto planning boards or as a "stand-alone" set of tactics
- Modify or update breakthrough planning boards and mission tree if required

Tools and References

- Seven QC (see "tools" section in the appendix)
- Tree diagram

Fig. 27: Planning Tree Diagram for Identifying Tactics to Achieve Breakthrough Objectives

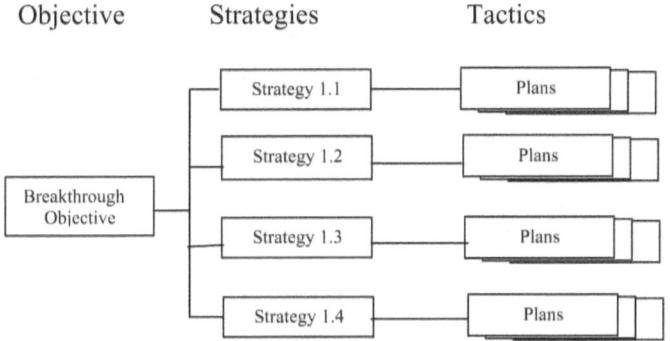

Tools and References to Use for Developing Breakthrough Tactics

- Fig. 28: Contingency Diagram Sheet

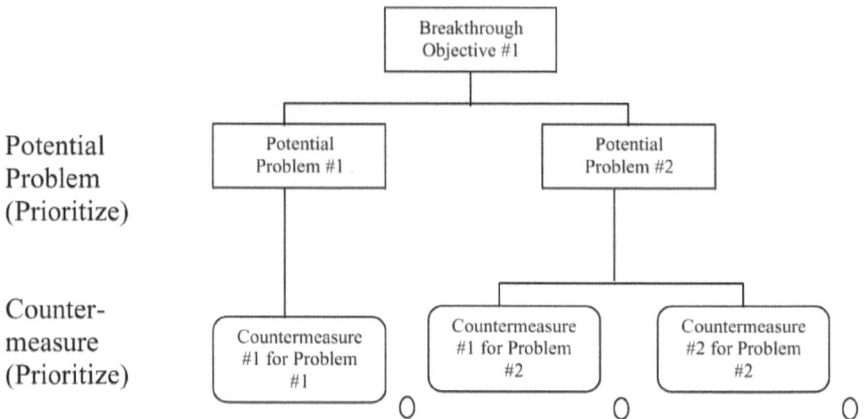

- Table 9: Example of a Narrowing (Decision-making) Matrix Sheet

Tactics	Effective	Efficient	Total
Strategy 1.1			
1.1.1 Tactic 1			
1.1.2 Tactic 2			
1.1.3 Tactic 3			
1.1.4 Tactic 4			
1.1.5 Tactic 5			
Strategy 1.2			
1.2.1 Tactic 1			
1.2.2 Tactic 2			
1.2.3 Tactic 3			
1.2.4 Tactic 4			
1.2.5 Tactic 5			

Strategy 1.3			
1.3.1 Tactic 1			
1.3.2 Tactic 2			
1.3.3 Tactic 3			
1.3.4 Tactic 4			

The weighting criteria generally used for assessing the above is:

High (H) = 9; Medium (M) = 3; Low (L) = 1

- Catchball: D/OMT    Project Teams
  Natural Work Groups

- Table 10: Linkages Matrix Sheet

Dept. Project/ Plans	Dept. A	Dept B	Dept. C
Project/Plan 1.1			
Project/Plan 1.2			
Project/Plan 1.3			
Project/Plan 1.4			

- Table 11: Accountability Matrix Sheet

ACTION	PROCESS	PROJECT/PROCESS OWNER
1.1 action plan	Process X	X process owner
1.2 action plan	Process Y	Y process owner
1.3 action plan	Process Z	Z process owner

Note: The concept of process ownership runs throughout the organization. Some of these action plans will involve people at the management level, and some may involve people at the supervisory level. The accountability for each action plan usually falls to the individual whose process is most impacted by the outcome of the plan.

Expected Outputs

The outputs of this phase are the completed and finalized breakthrough plans. Table 12 & Fig. 30 show two alternatives for recording plans.

Table 12: Example A: "Stand-alone" Plans Sheet

Business/Dept.	Manager		Date
Objective	Target		
Owner:			
Strategies/Plans	Perf. Meas.	Owner	Completion Date

Legend: Perf. Meas. = performance measures

Example B: All Tactics Added to Breakthrough Planning Boards

Fig. 29:   Example of a Planning Tree

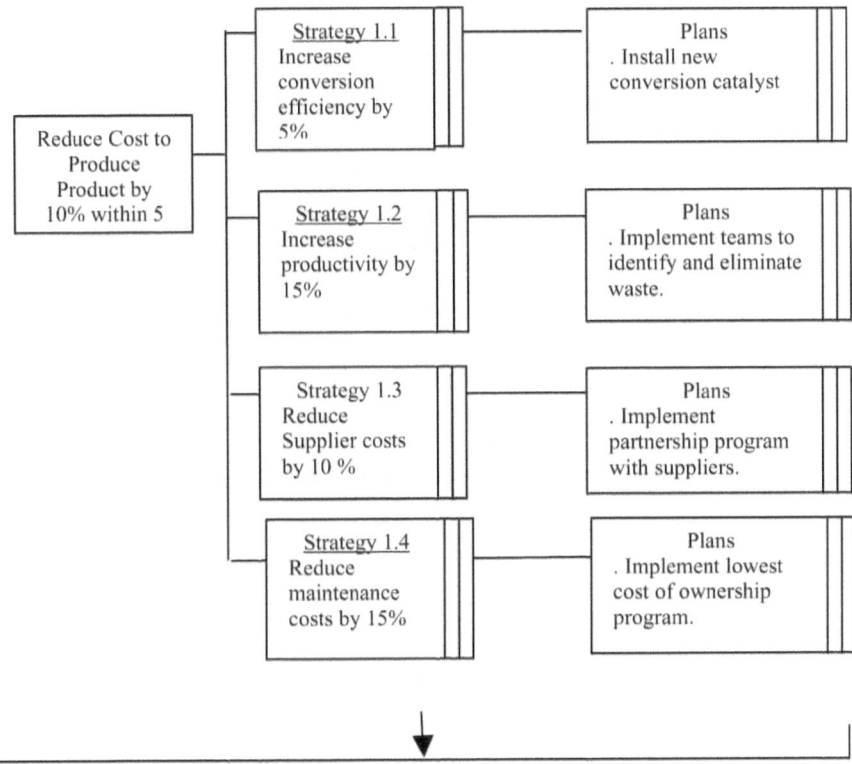

Fig. 30:   Example of a Filled-in Breakthrough Planning Board with Targets Finalized

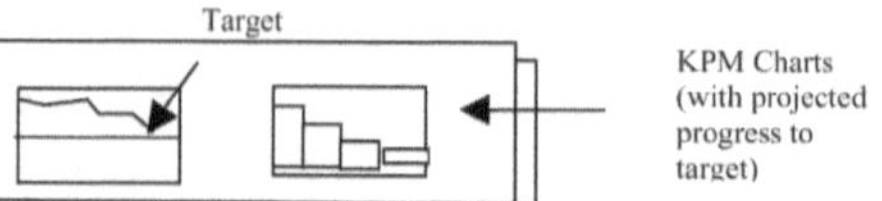

Objective: Reduce Cost to Produce Product by 12% within 5 yrs. Formula: Sum of all costs - Marketing			Target				KPM Charts (with projected progress to target)
Coordinator: Produce Product Process Owner							
Strategy	Owner	PM	Schedule Yr. 1 2 3 4 5				
1. Increase conversion efficiency by 5%	Build and modify owner	Efficiency	-----------------				
2. Increase productivity by 10%	Produce product owner	Productivity	------------------------				
3. Reduce Supplier costs by 15%	Utilize Assets owner	Supply costs	-------------------------				
4. Reduce maintenance costs by 17%	Maintain plant owner	Maintenance costs	-----------------				

Potential Pitfalls

Neglecting to ensure that:

- The people who are most knowledgeable at the tactical level and those who will have to implement the plans are involved in developing the tactics (with goals) and deciding on the plans necessary to achieve the goals.

- Adequate catchball occurs vertically and cross-functionally to ensure that all necessary parties understand what is required, and that they are committed to the achievement of the plans.

- Sponsors and leaders do an adequate job of communicating their requirements with regard to targets and time frames for achieving the strategies.

- Sponsors and leaders provide sufficient resources, training and time for the teams and individuals to do an adequate job of developing tactics and plans.

Incremental Improvement

Introduction

Incremental improvement occurs when natural work groups get involved in identifying where they can contribute to the organization's key performance measures and breakthrough objectives.

Not everyone in the organization will have been identified as a key contributor to the breakthrough objective(s). It is still important, however, that everyone be involved in incremental improvement in their areas and contribute to improving the organization's overall performance. In the incremental improvement component, a considerable amount of catchball occurs between natural work groups and the D/OMT leadership to determine process improvements and improvement goals and to finalize improvement targets.

Expectation

It is important to note here that all work groups, on at least an annual basis, are expected to work towards improving the performance of at least one of their key processes. The selection of the key process and the key performance measure is based on the direction (via a set of selection criteria) that is set out annually by the D/OMT. This criterion is developed by the D/OMT by looking at breakthrough objectives, potential improvement objectives and key department performance measures.

Inputs

The following inputs will be used as a set of criteria for natural work groups to use to select which key process they will be working on.

- Department breakthrough objectives
- Potential improvement objectives
  - Use non-breakthrough objectives identified in phase three
- Mission/vision element KPMs
- Control systems for key organizational work processes
  - Includes accountabilities and QI-* and PI-* measures
  - Managing daily work (QC)
- QI = quality indicator
- PI = process indicator

Incremental Improvement
Key Action One: Support the Development of Improvement Plans and Goals

Introduction

In key action one, the D/OMT develops prioritization criteria by combining break-through objectives, key performance measures and potential improvement targets from the previous phase. Catchball is used to communicate the prioritization criteria and identify the following factors with work groups and project teams:

- Key processes to be worked on in the coming year

- Improvement goals for selected processes

- Any new or existing projects that require significant capital or human resources

Tools and References

- Catchball

D/OMT      Natural Work Groups

- Table 13: Example of an Improvement Plan Sheet

Business/Dept. Mission Element/Objective Coordinator:			Manager Fiscal Yr KPM/Target		Date
Process	Quality Indicator	Target/ Limits	Improvement Plans	Owner	Review/ Compl.

Incremental Improvement
Key Action Two: Consolidate and Finalize
Improvement Tactics

Introduction

During this key action, the D/OMT sums up all contributions (process-improvement goals and plans for achieving breakthrough targets) from natural work groups and project teams—a clear trail of what people are working on, and how their efforts align with and impact on D/OMT key performance measures, is essential to implementation success in the next phase.

Tools and References

- D/OMT   ←—⊕→   Natural Work Groups

- Table 14: Example of an Improvement Plan Sheet

Key Work Process	Owner	KPM/Obj. Affected	Functions/ Groups	Man-hours Required	$ Required	External Help Needed
1.						
2.						
3.						
4.						
5.						
6.						

Legend: KPM = key performance measure

Obj. = objective

Expected Outputs

The Improvement plan guide is the primary output of this component.

Fig. 31:   Sample Sheet of Improvement Plan Guide

Business/Department			Manager			Date	
Mission Element/Objective Coordinator:			KPM/Target				
Process	Quality Indicator	Target/	Improvement Plans	Owner	Review/ Completion		
Operate Plant	----- -----	-------- --------	----------------------------- ---------------------------	---- ----	-------- --------		
Build and Modify	----- -----	-------- --------	----------------------------- ---------------------------	---- ----	-------- --------		
Maintain Plant	----- ----	-------- --------	----------------------------- ---------------------------	---- ----	-------- --------		

Legend: KPM = key performance measures

Potential Pitfalls

- Not stratifying the department's key performance measures down to measures that are meaningful to the natural work groups
- An existing culture that makes natural work groups fearful of becoming involved in making improvements or having measures set against their performance
- Natural work groups not trained in or familiar with identifying their key processes, developing control systems and developing performance measures

Phase Four: Implement and Review Progress

Introduction

Once plans are developed and finalized, they need to be implemented. This phase of MI ensures that performance expectations are clearly understood by all individuals involved in breakthrough and improvement plans, and that progress is monitored and supported.

Note: Progress reviews are conducted on a frequent basis (that is, daily, weekly, monthly, or quarterly).

Fig. 32:   Managing Improvement Process with Implement and Review Progress Highlighted

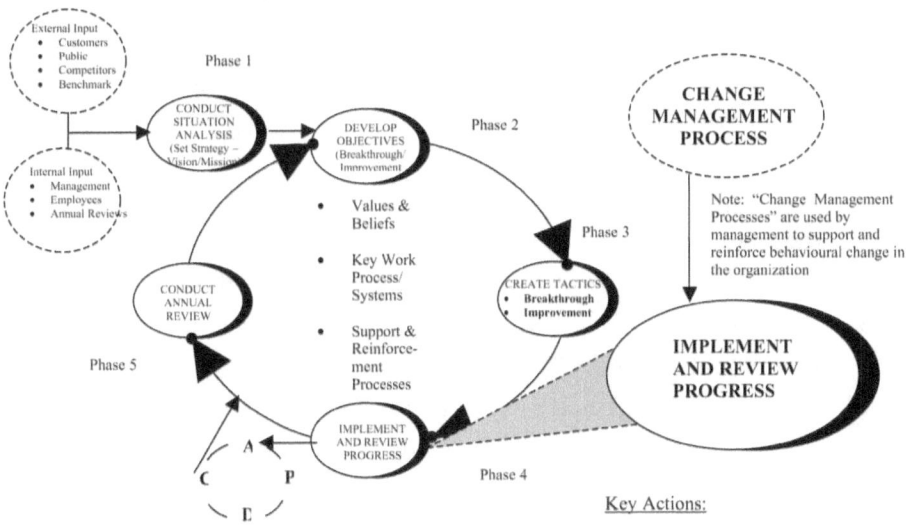

Key Actions:

1. Ensure that support structures are in place and kick-off plan is implemented
2. Promote Progress
3. Conduct Progress Reviews

Introduction

During the implementation and review progress phases, the D/OMT members do not usually implement plans. Instead, their role has more to do with ensuring that all the necessary training, support structures and resources are in place. They also need to provide the necessary coaching, support and reinforcement. This is imperative for those who have the job of implementing the plans.

This is where it becomes critical that the D/OMT understands what is required to ensure that all the components of an improvement system are in place, and that the organization's leaders have the tools, skills and knowledge necessary to ensure that motivation and support occur.

Purpose

The D/OMT role during the implementation and review progress phases of MI is:

- To ensure that:
  - The appropriate skills and knowledge (training) is available for the main role players
  - Support structures are in place
  - Communication systems are understood and being used
  - D/OMT members understand and fulfill their roles in providing support and reinforcement
- To communicate finalized plans to employees and ensure performance expectations are clearly understood by all
- To provide support and reinforce implementation efforts
- To review progress of plans toward achieving improvement targets and breakthrough objectives
- To conduct and/or coach others to conduct root-cause analysis

Inputs

The primary inputs for this phase are as follows:

- Change management skills and knowledge
- Department mission tree, objectives and target charts

- Breakthrough plans
  - Planning boards for each breakthrough objective
- Improvement plans

Key Action One: Kick-off Plans

Introduction

In key action one, the D/OMT ensures that all the conditions are in place for ensuring that people can achieve the plans and goals to which they are committed. The D/OMT should also be developing and executing a kick-off plan that will communicate organizational expectations to all departmental employees. The following specifics are generally included:

- Plan for needed training and where and when it is available
- Access to technical support and coaching
- Breakthrough and improvement objectives
- People accountable for implementation
- Timelines for completion
- Time for reviews to occur
- Processes to follow (problem-solving process, project process, control systems, etc.)
- Clear definitions of expectations (from employees and from management)

Tools and References

- Table 15: Sample Communication Strategy Format

Business/Department	Manager	Date
Purpose	Attendees	Place
Information	Who Communicates	Method of Communication

Key Action Two: Promote Progress

Introduction

Key Action Two involves creating an atmosphere conducive to improvement. The following activities will:

- Ensure that people have the skills and knowledge for making improvements
- Put in place structures that support people in their efforts to make improvements (for example, coaches or team sponsors)
- Help to identify and remove barriers during implementation of plans
- Reinforce efforts through informal reviews and meetings with implementers at strategic points in plans
- Ensure current and visible monitoring systems are displayed

Tools and References

- Technique: "Management by Walking About" (MBWA)
- Department mission tree and related charts
- Breakthrough planning boards

Key Action Three: Conduct Progress Reviews

Introduction

Monthly and quarterly reviews ensure that plans are progressing, deviations are corrected, targets and plans are changed if required, and employees are supported and reinforced for their efforts. The D/OMT should complete the following activities.

- Assess breakthrough plans:
    - Review progress against plans, performance measures and milestones of each breakthrough plan
    - Diagnose problems and develop corrective action plans
    - Review progress of plans with BMT on a quarterly basis to communicate problems or barriers that require additional resources
- Assess progress of improvement plans:
    - Review indicators
    - Check on level of employee involvement

Tools and References

- Cause analysis (see following example)

Expected Outputs

The outputs for conducting progress reviews are updated plans, measurement charts and planning boards.

Fig. 33:   Example of a Cause Analysis Chart

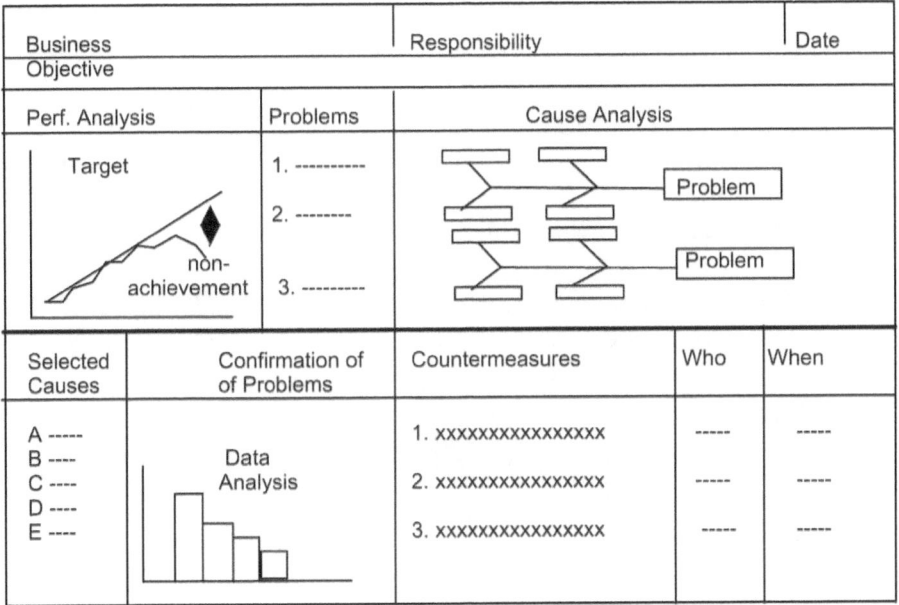

Potential Pitfalls

- Management fails to provide adequate coaching and support to the teams
- Teams do not assess their performance and document their learning for others (don't develop team storyboards)

Note: It should be noted how catchball has been played at each phase. Targets are initially set at a higher level in the organization, which are then passed down the organization. Those who need to implement the plans do a more in-depth study to see what they can actually do, and then these plans and new targets are rolled back up the organization. This process continues until the targets, time frames and accountabilities are firmed up and a reasonable expectation of meeting same is in place.

Phase Five: Annual Review

Introduction

The annual review phase causes the D/OMT to reflect on results achieved in the past year. It captures key learning from ongoing progress reviews, identifies system problems and provides recommendations for improvements.

The annual review is not just about management reviewing what they have done for the year. It also includes ensuring that they (management) learn how to plan better, and instituting all the systemic elements that will ensure that their organization is learning and improving. This includes:

- Information systems for capturing what teams and individuals have learned during the course of the year as they developed and implemented plans (both what worked well and what needs improving)
- Communication systems for passing this learning on to others
- Assurance that key learning is replicated in other areas of the organization (where appropriate)
- Removal of the barriers associated with "not-invented-here" types of thinking

Note: Some organizations have found that their greatest competitive advantage has come from their in-depth studies of mistakes they have made without pointing the finger or blaming someone.

Phase Five: Annual Review

Fig. 34:   Managing Improvement Process with Annual Review Highlighted

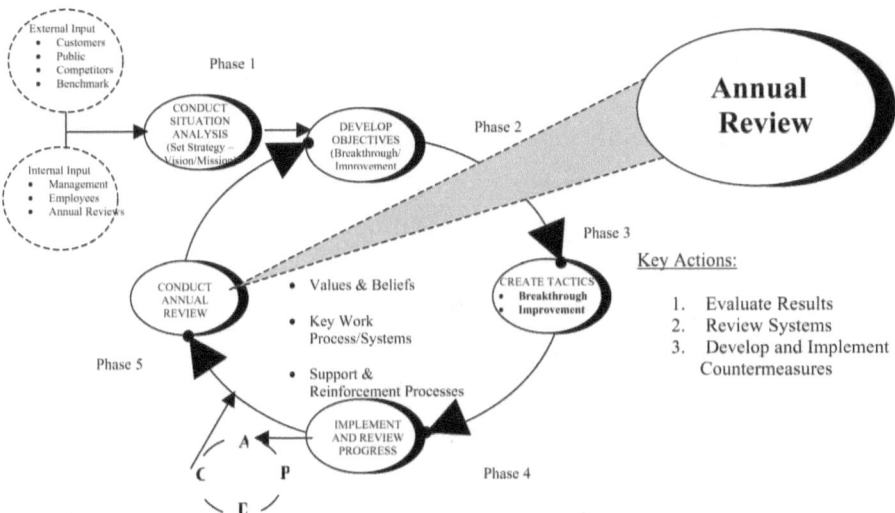

Note: It is important to understand that Managing Improvement is a learning cycle. In fact, it is a tool to help management improve their organizational planning and execution abilities. Therefore, after a number of cycles, the performance measures for management in regard to Managing Improvement are:

- Objective target set versus target reached
- Time frame set versus time frame met
- Resources and time used to conduct planning, execution and reviews

Purpose

The primary purposes of the annual review are (1) to increase the organization's effectiveness in planning and implementation, (2) to increase future ability to contribute to long-term objectives and (3) to standardize improvements through process control systems.

Inputs

The following items identify inputs to the annual review phase.

- Cause analysis sheets
  - Based on monthly or quarterly progress milestones and project completion reviews
- Key work process control systems reviews
- Tools used for the evaluation of systems
  - Criteria for self-assessment (such as systems matrices, ABC analysis, causal loop diagrams and cause-and-effect diagrams)
  - External criteria based on Malcolm Baldridge Award criteria, National Quality Institute criteria, Deming Awards criteria
  - Internal assessments—team assessments as shown in their cause analysis sheets

Key Action One: Evaluate Results

Introduction

Evaluating results involves the following activities:

- Reviewing breakthrough objectives and the contribution of key strategic areas and identifying reasons for deviation from the projected target (favourable or unfavourable deviations)
- Diagnosing problems and initiating development of corrective plans and countermeasures
- Reviewing improvement targets (key performance measures) and the level of employee involvement and contribution
- Evaluating progress toward the mission and long-term objectives

Tools and References

- Table 16: Sample of an Annual Review Sheet

ANNUAL REVIEW	Business	Responsibility	Date
Objective		Target	Owner
Strategies	Actual Performance vs. Target	Analysis of Deviations	Implications For Next Planning Cycle

Key Action Two: Review Systems

Introduction

This part of the annual review evaluates the Continuous Improvement system. It includes evaluating:

- The organization's ability to learn and to pass on its learning
- The D/OMT's ability to use the MI process itself. This includes assessing the quality of planning (that is, accomplishments relative to strategies and desired results) in order to increase the accuracy of future planning and the ability to contribute to long-term objectives
- The organization's ability to capture this learning in the form of systems that set and maintain the new standards
- Analyzing performance against self-assessment and external criteria

Tools and References

- Systems matrix
- Causal loop diagrams
- ABC analysis
- National Quality Institute criteria, Malcolm Baldridge Awards criteria and the Deming Awards criteria

Key Action Three: Develop and Implement Countermeasures

Introduction

The assessment of results and evaluation of systems identifies where countermeasures need to be developed and implemented to ensure continued progress towards long-term objectives and incremental improvement. These countermeasures need to link back to process-control systems at the appropriate level in the organization such that accountabilities and control points are established.

The D/MOI:

- Identifies implications for situation analysis in the next planning cycle
- Recommends key control system changes to ensure standardization of achieved improvements, or identifies where to implement countermeasures identified in the reviews
- Communicates results and reviews countermeasures with the BMT, CFMT, project teams and natural work groups

Tools and References

- Table 17: An Example of a Countermeasures Sheet

Business Element/Objective	Responsibility Target	Date Owner

Analysis (use the appropriate tool)			
Process	Countermeasure	Who	When

- Annual review form (sample as shown in "Expected Outputs")
- Process control systems (sample as illustrated in "Expected Outputs")
- Catchball

D/OMT		- Project Teams
BMT • CFMT		- Natural Work Groups

Expected Outputs

Outputs for this phase include the completed annual review form and standardized control systems.

Table 18: A Sample Completed Annual Review Sheet

ANNUAL REVIEW	Business	Responsibility	Date
Objective 1.0 Reduce Cost to Produce by		Target 12% in five years	Owner Operate Plant Process Owner
Strategies	Actual Performance Vs. Target	Analysis of Deviations	Implications For Next Planning Cycle
1. Increase conversion by 5%	0 %	Delivery of new catalyst delayed 3 months	Send person to catalyst supplier to help in expediting delivery
2. Increase productivity by 10%	5 %	On target as per schedule	No implications
3. Reduce Supplier Costs by 15%	5 %	Ahead of schedule (anticipate 15% improvement)	Work with suppliers to ensure quality of supplies
4. Reduce Maintenance costs by 17%	10 %	Ahead of schedule	Concerns re long-term cost of ownership problems due to reduced maintenance (Intend to increase preventive (PM) schedule)

- Fig. 35: Sample Modified Control Systems Sheet

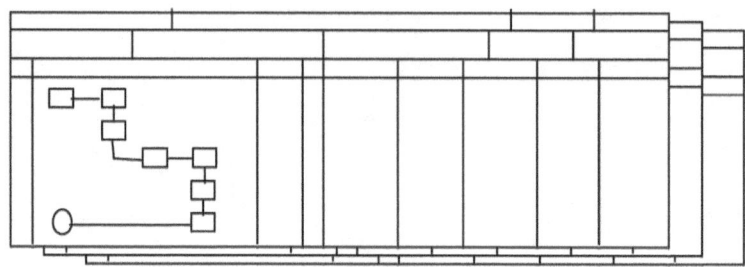

Potential Pitfalls

- Failure of the D/OMT members to ensure that the implementation teams analyzed and documented their learning as they developed and implemented their plans

- Failure to ensure that systems are in place for communicating and replicating this learning throughout the organization

- Failure by the D/OMT to do a thorough analysis of what worked and what didn't work

- Failure to understand and quantify the effect of the strategies and tactics on the long-term objectives

- Failure to build the learning into the existing or newly developed control systems such that long-term accountabilities are identified and control points instituted

Summary

Table 19: A Quick Reference Summarizing the MI Process

Phase	Steps			
1. Conduct Situation Analysis	1. Collect and Review Data 2. Assess Impact to BMT and CFMT Objectives 3. Develop Mission/Vision	• BMT Long-Term Objectives • BMT Mission and Vision • CFMT Long-Term Objectives • Annual Reviews	• Mission Tree • Strategic Areas of Improvement (Pareto Charts) • Element KPM Charts	• 7 Management Tools • 7 QC Tools • Surveys • Quality/System Assessment Tools
2. Develop Objectives	1. Create Objectives 2. Prioritize and Select Breakthrough Objectives 3. Finalize Targets	• BMT Long-Term Objectives • CFMT Long-Term Objectives • Pareto Analysis • Key Work Process Control Systems	• Department Mission (modified) • KPM Charts (projected) • Breakthrough Planning Boards	• 7 Management Tools • Y Matrix • Objectives Matrix • Catchball

3. Create Tactics	• Department Mission/Vision Tree & KPM Charts • Breakthrough Planning Boards • Key Work Process Control Systems	**Breakthrough** 1. Develop Plans for Each Objective 2. Finalize Breakthrough Plans **Improvement** 1. Develop Improvement Plans 2. Consolidate/Finalize Goals	• Breakthrough Planning Boards (modified) • Breakthrough Plans • Improvement Plans	• Catchball • 7 Mgmt. Tools Matrix: Work Process to Objectives Linkages; • Accountability; Prioritization Criteria; Target Estimate
4. Implement and Review Progress	• Depart Mission • Breakthrough Planning Boards • Improvement Plans	1. Kickoff Plans 2. Promote Progress 3. Conduct Progress Reviews	• Updated Plans & Planning Boards • Cause Analysis	• Kick-off Strategy • MBWA • Cause Analysis Charts
5. Annual Review	• Cause Analysis Charts • System Criteria • Key Work Process Control Systems	1. Evaluate Results 2. Review Systems 3. Develop and Implement Counter-measures	• Annual Review Form • Counter-measures & Modified or Standardized Control Systems	• Annual Review Form • Cause Analysis Charts • Counter-measures sheet

TOOLS SECTION

Simple Tools

Fig. 36:   Simple QC Tools

Check Sheet

Type of Causes	# of Causes	Total #
A	1111 11	7
B	1111	5
C	111	3
D	1	1

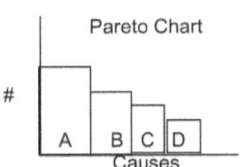

Pareto Chart

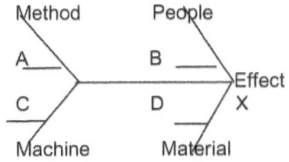

Cause-and-Effect Diagram

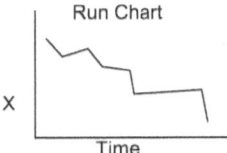

Run Chart

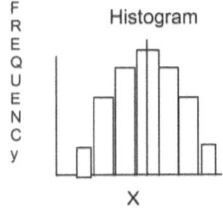

Histogram

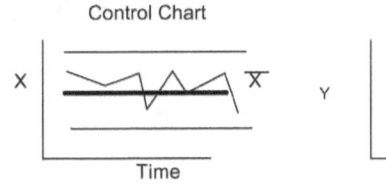

Control Chart   Scatter Diagram

The Management Tools

Affinity Diagram

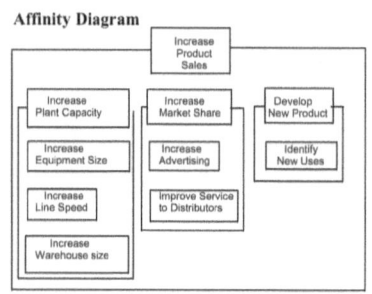

Relations Diagram

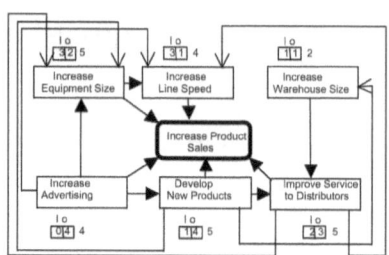

Tree Diagram

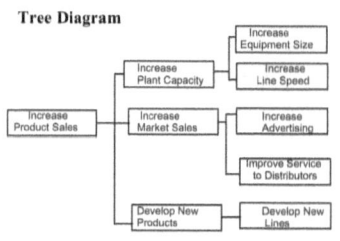

Matrix Diagram

	Cost effectiveness	Ease of implementation	Effectiveness	Ease of doing	Total
• Increase Equipment Size	L	M	M		7
• Increase Line Speed	M	H	M		15
• Increase Advertising	L	M	H		13
• Improve Service to	H	H	H		27
• Identify New Uses	M	H	L		13

Measurement Matrix

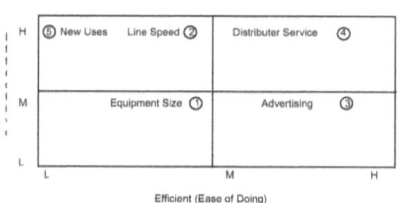

Contingency Diagram

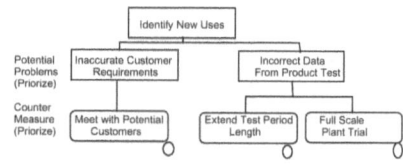

Arrow Diagram

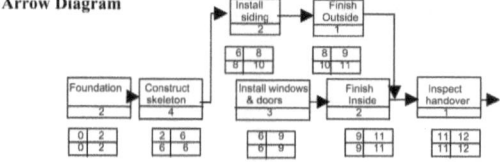

Creativity Tools

- Reversing assumptions
- Forcing associations
- Making comparisons
- Discovering Other points of view
- Exploring Outrageous ideas
- Using Guided imagery

Appendix A

Situation Analysis

Situation Analysis at the BMT Level

Introduction to Situation Analysis in Terms of D/OMT versus BMT

The Situation Analysis step for a department or operational team (D/OMT), although requiring a significant amount of data gathering and analysis, is relatively straightforward if leaders have done a thorough job of developing business objectives. Provided all the data-gathering systems are in place and functioning, this step requires perhaps one month on the part of the D/OMT. Phase one is primarily focused on setting up these data-collection systems. Then ongoing Situation Analyses become part of the annual review. This is a tactical activity.

The Situation Analysis for the overall business organization (particularly initially) requires a much more in-depth analysis. This helps the BMT establish a solid foundation for strategy development. Initial completion of the Situation Analysis requires substantial effort—approximately nine months—to (1) create an integrated fact base, (2) identify initial strategic issues and (3) develop a value-maximizing strategy for the organization.

Thereafter, the BMT updates its business strategy on an ongoing basis (for example, annually and/or when changes occur). An assessment of the organization's position is updated annually to refresh the fact base and renew strategic issues and/or alternatives. This is more of a strategic activity.

Situation Analysis:
For-Profit versus Not-For-Profit Organizations

An example for a manufacturing organization is given at the end of this section. The same thought process and set of key actions apply for "not-for-profit" and service organizations.

Synonyms for Situation Analysis

Another term for Situational Analysis is the "Strength, Weakness, Opportunities and Threats" (SWOT) analysis. The SWOT analysis is typically concerned with both an external and internal look. For further information on the SWOT analysis, see *Concepts of Strategic Management*, Fifth Edition, by Fred R. David, 1995.

External Analysis: Opportunities and threats (OT) represent the external issues facing the organization.

Internal Analysis: Strengths and weaknesses (SW) represent the internal issues facing the organization.

How Does a Business Plan Fit with Managing Improvement?

The business plan comes as a result of the Situation Analysis and serves as a management tool to guide strategy implementation and monitor performance. It summarizes the BMT's business strategy, specifies performance measures (both operating and financial), and clarifies the major objectives and targets required to achieve the business strategy. Business plan development occurs during phases two and three of the (MI) process.

Organizational Performance Measures

Objectives, goals and performance measures are fundamental to the implementation of strategy and to the effective use of the MI process. Most organizations measure their performance based on financial performance alone. Although these measures tell the organization how they did in the past, they do not indicate what its performance will be in the future. Financial measures are *lagging* indicators (what has already happened); organizations need good *leading* indicators (what is likely to happen in the future).

In their book *The Balanced Scorecard*, Kaplan and Norton (1996) give four levels of measures that an organization should have or develop. They are:

1. *Financial*
2. *Customer*
3. *Process*
4. *Learning and improvement*

These metrics are hierarchical in that the financial measures are the survival measures, or lagging measures, which reveal how well the organization has done in the past. They do not necessarily indicate how well the organization will do in the future.

The customer measures, which are next in the hierarchy, can be both lagging and leading measures in that they reveal what is presently important to the customers. They can also be structured to reveal what is changing and likely to influence organizational results in the future. Changes in the customer measures are likely to indicate what the financial measures will look like in the future.

Process measures, the third level of the hierarchy, indicate the performance of the organization's key processes. A focus on the efficiency and effectiveness of the organizational processes is essential. They are leading measures for determining the future performance of both customer perceptions and, eventually, the financial indicators.

The last measure in this hierarchy (learning and improvement) has to do with the performance of the employees of the organization. The level of skills and motivation of the employees ultimately impact on all other levels in the hierarchy.

In the case of "for-profit" organizations, the top measures, or *survival* measures, are usually very clear. If the organization is not able to generate a profit over a sustained period of time (generally fairly short), it will cease to exist. In "not-for-profit" organizations, the survival measures are less clear. The other three levels of the measurement hierarchy are essentially the same for both types of organizations. The challenge for the "not-for-profit" organizations is to determine and define their survival measures.

Economic Profit (EP)

The latest financial measure, a measure which has shown a good correlation with business performance, is termed economic profit (EP) or Economic Value Added (EVA).

Economic profit, or Economic Value Added is defined as operating profits less the cost of all of the capital employed to produce those earnings (Stewart 1991).

EVA® is a Registered Trademark of Stern Stewart & Co. (in the field of financial and incentive consulting)

and of EVA Dimensions LLC (in the field of data and valuation analytics and investment management)

Topic	Page
Key Actions for Conducting A Situation Analysis at the Business Level	
Manufacturing Example	

Topic	Page
Key Actions for Conducting A Situation Analysis at the Business Level	
Manufacturing Example	
Key Action 1: Assess Current Strategy	
Key Action 2: Identify Strategic Issues	
Key Action 3: Formulate Alternative Strategies	
Key Action 4: Select a Strategy/Strategies	
Key Action 5: Develop Mission and Vision	

Key Actions for Conducting a Situation Analysis at the Business Level

Introduction

Setting up the data-gathering systems, then collecting and analyzing the data, is a foreboding task, especially initially. Typically, a special task force referred to as the "Business Analysis Team" (BAT) is set up to accomplish this work. When first setting up the data-gathering systems, this is also an appropriate action for the D/OMT.

The Business Analysis Team (BAT)

During the SWOT analysis, the BMT establishes and works closely with a BAT. The BAT performs extensive information gathering and analysis for BMT review or decision-making during the business plan development phase.

Definition of a Business Unit

A business unit is one that can stand on its own financially. It has supplies, suppliers and paying customers, and it can bring value to the overall organization without having to be supported by the rest of the organization.

Inputs

The following list identifies the primary inputs required for Situational Analysis.

- Corporate
  - Vision, values and objectives (VVO)
  - Mission
- Market plan sub-process information
  - Intelligence or synthesized information
- Database networks
- Information sources
  - Operational plants
  - Research and development (R&D)
  - Technology centers
  - Sales
  - Marketing
  - Strategic research services

Relationship of Situation Analysis to Managing Improvement

The following depicts the key actions that are required for conducting a Situational Analysis at the business level.

Fig. A-1: Managing Improvement Process with Conduct Situation Analysis Highlighted

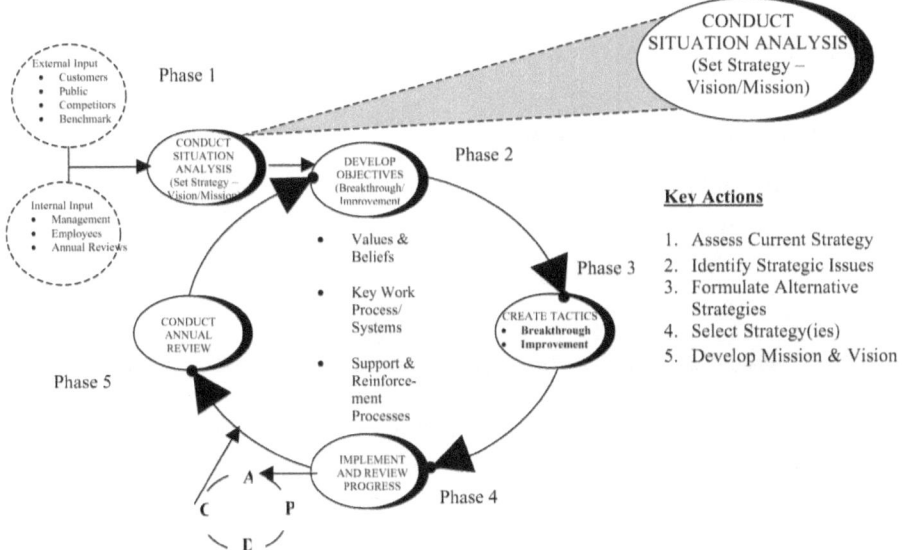

Phase One: Conduct Situation Analysis

Conducting a Situation Analysis at the business or corporate level involves looking at strategic issues. In this case, "strategic issues" means looking at the fundamental issues of why the business exists, who it intends to serve, what it wants to become and by when. In addition, it needs to establish some boundaries about what it does not want to do or become. There are five key actions associated with conducting Situation Analysis at the business level, and they are:

Key Actions:

1. Assess current strategy
2. Identify strategic issues
3. Formulate alternative strategies
4. Select strategy or strategies
5. Develop mission and vision

1. **Assess Current Strategy**	An assessment of the current strategy develops comprehensive information about current and future sources and drivers of value. It provides the BMT with a thorough understanding of: • The "best in class" organization and one's own organization's current and future value by product or service market segment under current strategies • Drivers of value in served markets • Capital value of the organization's current strategy • Insights regarding changes in current strategy which may lead to value improvement

2. Identify Strategic Issues	• Key strategic issues and performance-improvement issues are identified
	
	  - Value of the organization issues (from position assessment)
	
	  - Customer or client needs (from position assessment; customer matrix)
	
	  - Corporate issues (the organization management board's priorities; functional service initiatives)
	
	  - Annual review results
	
	• Issues are evaluated for improvement opportunities
	
	  - Develop or modify vision and mission indicators and/or long-term objectives and strategies (phases two and three)
	
	• Current strategy (i.e., business plan) is updated as required
	
	Note: In subsequent planning cycles, critical issues from an annual review or emerging changes to business position are analyzed for impact on, and modifications required to, the existing business plan (e.g., modified targets). However, on an annual basis, it is unlikely that issues will be of sufficient impact to seriously alter the business plan. Most issues would be resolved in the short—term (annual) plan, and little or no action would be required by the BMT.

3. Formulate Alternative Strategies	The objective of formulating alternative strategies is to develop strategic alternatives to the current business strategy, in each market segment, that are likely to create significantly more value. *Creativity* (out-of-box thinking, mental models, and process for innovation) is an essential factor during this key action.

4. Select Strategy or Strategies	In this key action, the BMT needs to determine the *value* of each strategic alternative. Alternatives are assessed for impact on the competitive environment, risk factors and potential to maximize value (rather than rates of return or shares, as in the past). This enables the BMT to select the highest-value business strategy for catchball with the organization's leadership team. Note: The agreed-to strategy becomes input for establishing strategic intent and competitive standard (i.e., the beginning of the business plan) in the next phase of MI.
5. Develop Vision & Mission	In phase one of MI, the BMT selected a value-maximizing strategic option. This phase of MI integrates the selected option with the organization's vision/mission, marking the start of the business plan. The purposes of this phase are to define strategic intent and set the competitive standard for the business—in essence, establish the vision/mission. Note: The vision/mission is not rigorously developed each year. Once established, it is reviewed annually and modified as required. Vision: See the "D/OMT" section in unit six for developing a mission/vision. Mission: A clear statement of purpose that indicates the chosen direction of the business. It describes: • Strategic focus • Products and services • Market/customer segments • Core competencies • Vertical integration

Manufacturing Example

Example situation analysis for
a manufacturer of a building
material

Key Action One: Assess Current Strategy

Introduction

An assessment of the current strategy develops comprehensive information about current and future sources and drivers of value. It provides the BMT with a thorough understanding of:

- The organization's and competitors' current and future economic profitability by product market segment under current strategies
- Industry and competitive drivers of economic profitability in served markets
- Capital value of the organization's current strategy
- Insights regarding changes in current strategy which may lead to value improvement

Sub-steps for Key Action One:

The procedure for completing the current strategy assessment involves the following seven steps:

1. *Product market segmentation* identifies appropriate product market segments for measuring profitability and competitive advantage.

2. *The organization's current profitability* identifies the organization's historic economic costs and profitability

3. *Current competitive position* determines the relative position of the organization and its competitors by product market segment regarding:

   a) Economic cost: lower capital cost/unit; lower operating cost/unit

   b) Differentiation: perceived superiority of the organization's current product offering relative to competitors (independent of price); surveying the organization's customers and non-customers to assess relative importance and fulfillment of major needs

4. *Current industry profitability:* determines historic industry profitability of the organization's market segments; analyzes industry characteristics to identify influences on current and future profitability

5. *The organization's and competitors' strategies:* establishes the organization's and competitors' current strategies and determines how they influence the organization's competitive position in the future

6. *Future industry profitability and competitive position:* estimates future expected growth and profitability in product market segments and establishes the organization's future differentiation and economic cost position relative to competitors

7. *The organization's current strategy valuation:* estimates the organization's future economic profit, determines the value of the organization's current strategy and identifies sources or key drivers of value creation

Tools and References

- Market intelligence database

  (for example, trends, customer needs, segmentation, structural analysis, market profitability, differentiation)

- Shared data network

  (for example, competitive manufacturing costs and technology)

- Competitive intelligence network

  (for example, competitive cost position, relative product performance, product differentiation, new product development)

- Fig. A-2: Bubble Chart

Organization versus Competitor Relative Price versus Cost Position

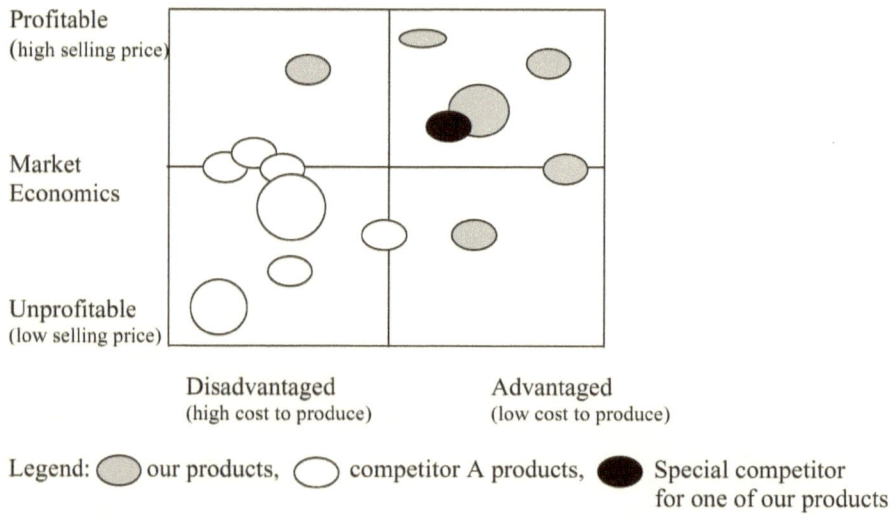

Legend: ⬭ our products, ◯ competitor A products, ⬤ Special competitor for one of our products

Note: Bubble charts are one way to show three dimensions of data in a flat 2D chart. The bubble area represents the third dimension to be displayed. For instance market size. The different colored bubbles represent different competitors.

Fig. A-3: Waterfall and Bar Charts

Organization versus Industry EP by Market Segment

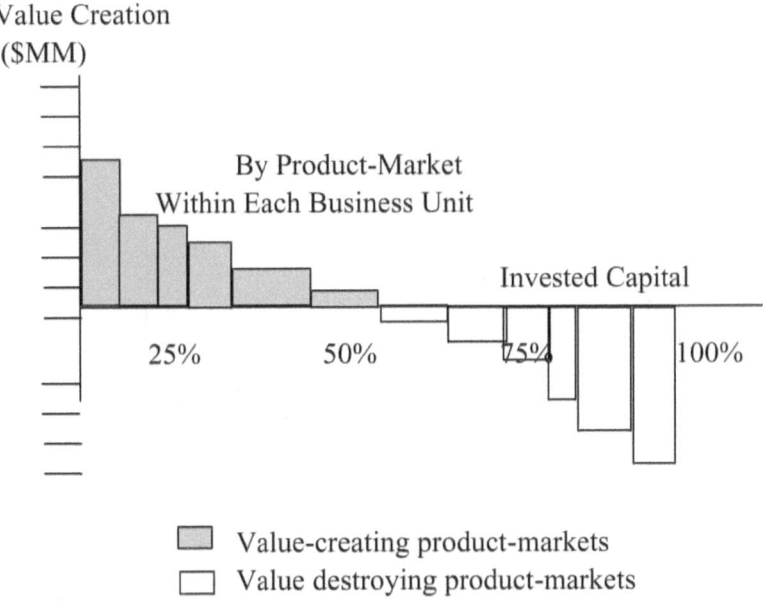

Value Creation
($MM)

By Product-Market
Within Each Business Unit

Invested Capital

25% 50% 75% 100%

▨ Value-creating product-markets
☐ Value destroying product-markets

Note: Waterfall charts show economic profit per unit versus volume for markets, products, or customers.

• Fig. A-4: Matrices, Tables or Spreadsheets

Product EP/Customer

Invoiced Customer	Product Name	Final Sales	Final Volume	EC/ unit	EP/ unit	EP
XXXXXXXX	XXXXXX	XXX	XXXX	XXXXX	XXX	XX
XXXXXXX	XXXXXX	XXX	XXXX	XXXXX	XXX	XX
XXXXXXX	XXXXXX	XXX	XXXX	XXXXX	XXX	XX
XXXXXXX	XXXXXX	XXX	XXXX	XXXXX	XXX	XX
XXXXXXX	XXXXXX	XXX	XXXX	XXXXX	XXX	XX
XXXXXXX	XXXXXX	XXX	XXX	XXXXX	XXX	XX
XXXXXXX	XXXXXX	XXX	XXX	XXXXX	XXX	XX

Legend: EC = economic cost; EP = economic profit

- Fig. A-5: Customer Matrix

Differentiation Position
(relative fulfillment of customer needs)

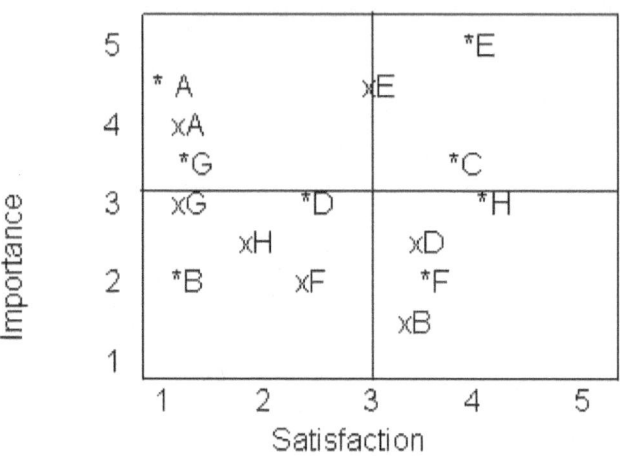

Legend: * = organization; x = competitor

- Fig. A-6: Using Organization and Competitor Strategy Documents

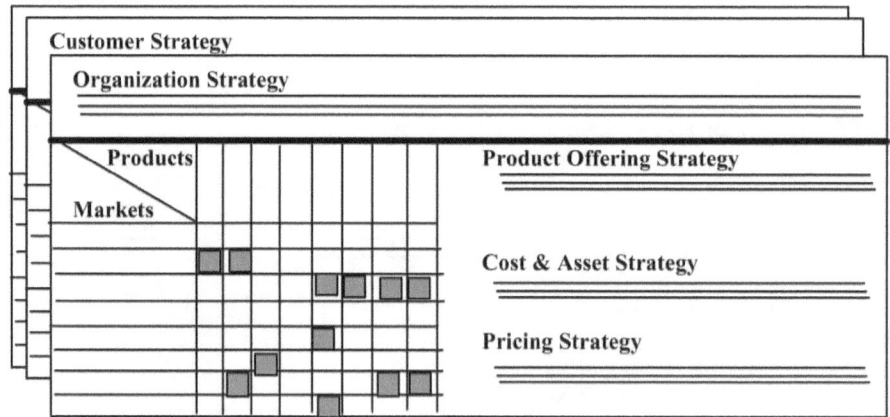

Key Action Two: Identify Strategic Issues

Activities and Outputs

The following activities occur in key action two:

- Key strategic issues and performance improvement issues are identified
  - Financial issues (from position assessment)
  - Customer needs (from position assessment; customer matrix)
  - Corporate issues (the organization's management board priorities; functional service initiatives)
  - Annual review results
- Issues are evaluated for improvement opportunities
  - Develop or modify vision and mission indicators and/or long-term objectives and strategies (phases two and three)
- Current strategy (i.e., business plan) is updated as required

Note: In subsequent planning cycles, critical issues from annual reviews or emerging changes to business positions or both are analyzed for impact on, and modifications required to, the existing business plan (for example, modified targets). However, on an annual basis, it is unlikely that issues will be of sufficient impact to seriously alter the business plan. Most issues would be resolved in the short-term (annual) plan, and little or no action would be required by the BMT.

Tools and References

Seven management tools (see "Tools" section)

Key Action Three: Formulate Alternative Strategies

Activities and Outputs

The object of formulating alternative strategies is to develop strategic alternatives to the current business strategy in each market segment that are likely to create significantly more value. As mentioned earlier, creativity, mental models, process for innovation) are helpful during this key action.

The following depicts how a tree diagram can be used to go from the selected alternative down to determining specific tactics to undertake.

Fig. A-7: Tree Diagram for Identifying Tactics for Each Alternative

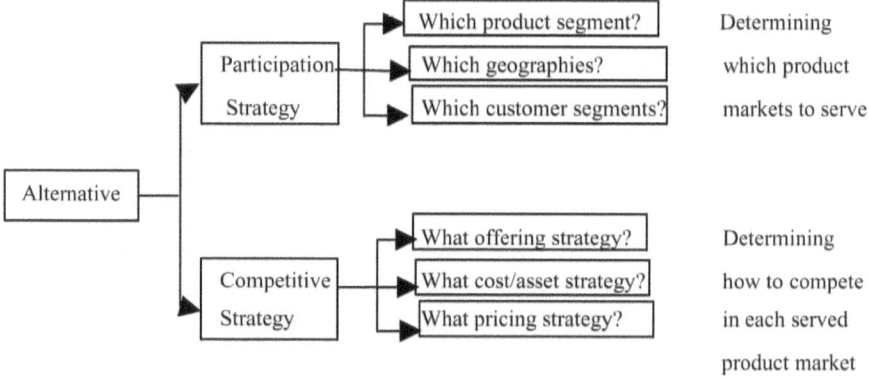

Tools and References

- Seven creativity tools (see "Tools" section)
- Seven management tools (see "Tools" section)

Key Action Four: Select a Strategy or Strategies

Introduction

In this key action, the BMT needs to determine the *value* of each strategic alternative. Alternatives are assessed for impact on the competitive environment, risk factors and potential to maximize value, rather than rates of return or shares as in the past. This enables the BMT to select the highest-value business strategy for catchball with the organization's leadership team.

Note: The agreed-to strategy becomes input for establishing strategic intent and competitive standard (that is, the beginning of the business plan) in the next phase of MI.

Tools and References

* Management tools

Fig. A-8: Using Criteria, Profit and Risk and Alternative Evaluation Matrices

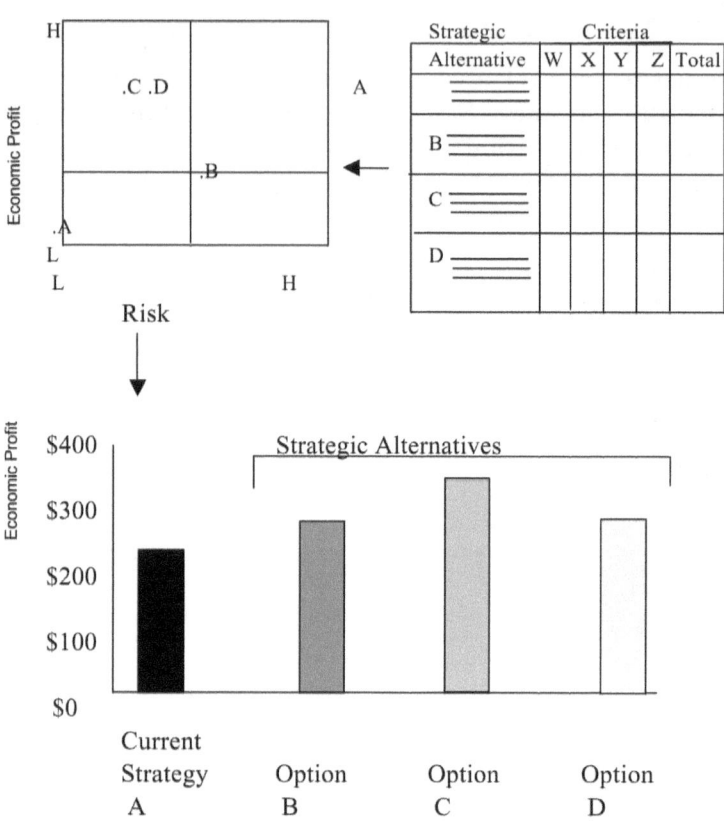

Situation Analysis Expected Outputs for Key Action Four

The expected outputs of Situation Analysis for this key action are listed below.

- ### Fig. A-9: Position Assessment Results

  For example: organization economic profit (EP) by segment; industry EP by segment; EP by customer within segment.

  Organization versus Industry EP by Market Segment

  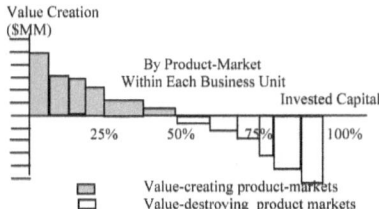

  Example of Detailed Competitive Analysis:

  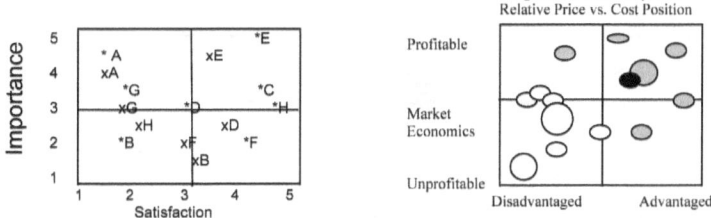

  Legend: * = organization; x = competitor; EP = economic profit

  Legend: ⬭ our products, ⬭ competitor A products, ⬤ Special competitor for one of our products

- Fig. A-10: An Example of Options Valuation

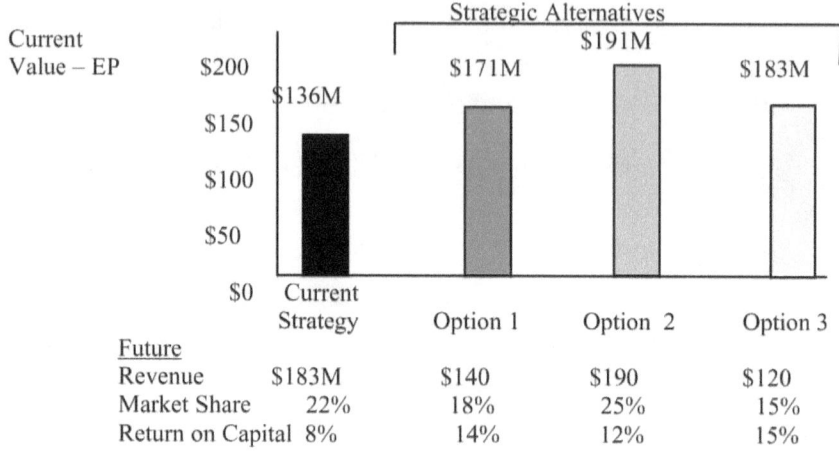

	Current Strategy	Option 1	Option 2	Option 3
Future				
Revenue	$183M	$140	$190	$120
Market Share	22%	18%	25%	15%
Return on Capital	8%	14%	12%	15%

- Fig. A-11: An Example of a Selected Strategic Option

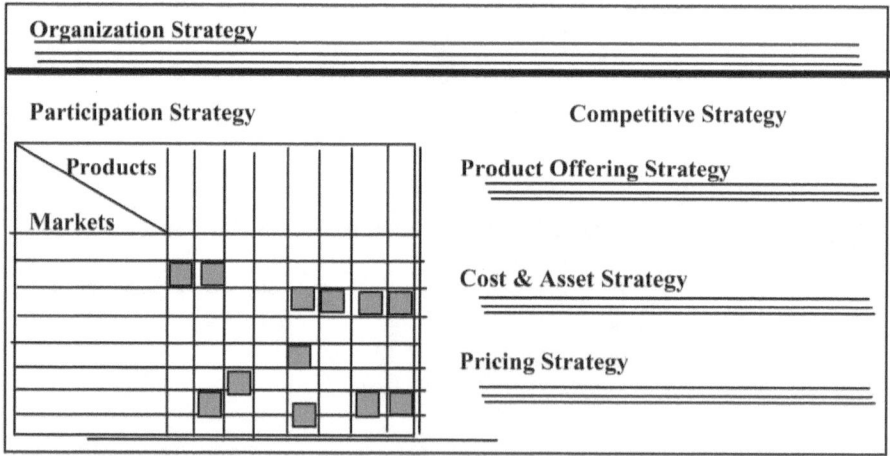

Potential Pitfalls during Situation Analysis Phase

- Forward movement without data on current situation
- Inability to achieve non-traditional, *innovative* thinking.

Key Action Five: Develop Vision and Mission

Introduction

In phase one of MI, the BMT selected a value-maximizing strategic option. This phase of MI integrates the selected option with the organization's vision and mission and marks the start of the business plan.

Purposes

The purposes of this phase are to define strategic intent and set the competitive standard for the business—in essence, it establishes the vision and mission.

Note: As said earlier, the vision and mission are not rigorously developed each year. Once established, they are reviewed annually and modified as required.

Mission Statement

A mission statement is a clear statement of purpose that indicates the chosen direction of the business. It describes:

- Strategic focus
- Products and services
- Market/customer segments
- Core competencies
- Vertical integration

Appendix B

Continuous

Improvement

Roles

Team Sponsor Performance Expectations

Broad Steps	Specific Actions	√
1. Provide Direction for the Team	• Identify clear objectives and goals. • Ensure that the goals/objectives are supported by reasons for improvement (data)	
2. Identify Team Participants	• Work with team leader to identify the team participants. • Agree with the team leader on facilitator involvement.	
3. Clarify Performance Expectations	• Performance expectations clarified with the team leader (performance checklist used). • Performance expectations clarified with the team facilitator. • Agree with the team and team leader on success criteria. • Gain agreement with the team leader on the sponsor involvement. • Set initial target, time frame with the team. • Communicate the team constraints. • Gain agreement with the team leader on the process to be used for problem solving and project management.	

4. Support the Team	<ul><li>Attend the first one or two meetings and ensure a smooth start for the team.</li><li>Conduct a review after the team sets a target, defines the opportunity and develops a project plan.</li><li>Conduct a review after the team completes root-cause analysis.</li><li>Play catchball with their people/team to ensure objectives can be supported by plans.</li><li>Conduct a review after the team completes the project, implements a control system and does a self-analysis.</li><li>Review all team meeting minutes and meet with the team leader and/or facilitator periodically.</li><li>Update the D/OMT on team progress and gain support where required.</li></ul>	
5. Recognize the Team	<ul><li>Give feedback to the team leader and team facilitator.</li><li>Give feedback to the team leader's and facilitator's supervisors.</li><li>Decide on team celebration (use team success criteria).</li></ul>	

Facilitator Performance Expectations

Broad Steps	Specific Actions	
1. Help Team Leader Prepare for Meetings	• Work with team leader to prepare the agenda. • Identify pitfalls and develop contingency plans. • Identify where content experts are required. • Identify what pre-work needs to be done. • Suggest appropriate tools and processes. • Decide on the fallback for decision making.	
2. Help the Team Leader & Members Focus on the Meeting	• Ensure meeting purpose and desired outcomes are clearly understood. • Ensure balanced participation. • Train/coach team members on QC tools.	
3. Strive for Consensus	• Defend team members from personal attack. • Use appropriate tools to help in consensus making. • Record people's ideas visibly.	
4. Keep the Meeting Moving	• Maintain a productive pace. • Check back with the group to get a sense of the pace and modify where appropriate.	
5. Ensure Action Items Are Identified in the Meeting	• Get agreement on actions and record them. • Help the group define the *how* for action items (where appropriate).	
6. Improve the Meeting Process	• Ask for and record the positives and areas for change in the meeting process.	

Project Team Leader Performance Expectations

Broad Steps	Specific Actions	
1. Select the Team	• Help select the team members.	

2. Define the Opportunity	• Do some pre-work (data collection on reasons for doing the project) to help the team get started.
	• Get help from the team facilitator and sponsor in getting a preliminary definition of the opportunity.
	• Develop a preliminary project plan and target with the team.
	• Lead the team to a successful first review with the sponsor to:
	  • Gain agreement on the opportunity statement, target and project plan
	  • Fill out the team storyboard	

3. Determine Present Situation	• Lead the team to analyze and understand the present situation.	
4. Analyze the Data	• Lead the team to analyze the opportunity from the first level of stratification to root cause.	
5. Develop Implementation Plans	• Lead the team to develop implementation plans. • Lead the team to develop contingency plans. • Work with the facilitator and/or sponsor to help the team to a successful review to gain support for the target, project plan, root-cause analysis and implementation plans. This includes a filled-out storyboard to this phase.	

6.	Implement Plans & Measure Data	• Coach and follow up with team members on the implementation of the plans. • Determine ways to help the team members identify barriers. • Work with the facilitator and/or sponsor to overcome these barriers.	
7.	Develop Control Systems	• Lead the team to develop control systems for the process. • Lead the team to develop and implement a communication/training plan for the installation of the control system. • Work with the coordinator and/or sponsor to lead the team to a successful review. • Lead the team to gain the agreement of the team sponsor that they have successfully completed the opportunity. Complete a simple communication tool for explaining the process that they have completed.	
8.	Recognize the Team	• Give performance feedback to team members, facilitator and supervisors. • Work with the sponsor or team members' supervisors to ensure the team members are recognized for their performance.	
9.	Overall	• Do pre-meeting planning (agenda & desired outcomes) for each meeting. • Do post-meeting assessment of each meeting.	

Team Member Performance Expectations

Broad Steps	Specific Actions	
1. Participate in Meetings	• Attend all of the meetings • Input ideas and solutions • Help and support other team members	
2. Complete Assignments Prior to Each Meeting	• Collect data • Interpret data and identify root cause • Prepare for sponsor reviews	
3. Communicate with Peers Who Are Not Part of the Team	• Communicate with peers what is happening on the team. • Get input from peers who are not on the team and bring this information back to the team.	

Bibliography

Ackoff, Russell, (from a talk given at the 10th Annual Conference GOAL/QPC conference held at the Weston Hotel in Boston, MA on November 8, 9 & 10th, 1993).

Akao, Yoji, Editor. *Hoshin Kanri: Policy Deployment for Successful TQM*. Portland, Oregon: Productivity Press, 1991.

Berger, Lance A. and Martin J Sikora. *The Change Management Handbook*. Irwin Professional Publishing, 1994.

The Bottom Line Group. *Adapt Bench Marking*. 1993.

Champy, James. *Reengineering Management*. HarperCollins, 1995.

Covey, Stephen. *Principle-Centered Leadership*. Summit Books, 1991.

Customer Window Process. Media, PA: Arbor, Inc., 1992.

Daniels, Aubrey C. *Performance Management Rx*. Tucker, GA: Performance Management Publications, 1989.

David, Fred R. *Concepts of Strategic Management*. Prentice Hall, Inc., 1995.

Davis, Brian L. et al. *Successful Manager's Handbook*. Personnel Decisions, 1996.

Deming, Edwards. *The New Economics*. Cambridge, MA: MIT Center for Advanced Study, 1993.

Hammer, Michael, and James Champy. *Reengineering the Corporation*. New York: Harper Business, 1993.

Imai, Masaaki. *Kaizen*. McGraw-Hill, Inc., 1986.

Johnston, Catharine G., and Mark J. Daniel. *Setting the Direction: Management by Planning*. Conference Board of Canada.

Kaplan, Robert. *The Balanced Scorecard*. Harvard Business, 1996.

Kubler-Ross, *Dr. Elizabeth, Adult Teaching Guide*, Scripture Press, December 1995 to February 1996.

Manganelli, Raymond L., and Mark M. Klein. The *Reengineering Handbook*. New York: Amacon, 1994.

Mintzberg, Henry. *The Rise and Fall of Strategic Planning*. New York: The Free Press, 1994.

Murgatroyd, S., and C. Morgan. *Total Quality Management and the School of London*. Open University Press, 1993.

Nadler, Gerald, and Shozo Hibino. *Breakthrough Thinking*. Prima Publishing & Communications, 1990.

National Quality Institute of Canada. *Quality Criteria*.

Porter, Michael, *Competitive Advantage: Creating and Sustaining Superior Performance*. New York: Free Press, 1985.

Senge, Peter. *The Fifth Discipline*. New York: Doubleday, 1990.

Stace, Doug, and Dexter Dunphy. *Beyond the Boundaries: Leading and Re-creating the Successful Enterprise*. Sydney: McGraw Hill, 1994.

Steward, G. Bennett III. *The Quest for Value*. HarperCollins, 1991.

Webster's New Twentieth Century Unabridged Dictionary, Second Edition, 1985

Index

www.ingramcontent.com/pod-product-compliance
Lightning Source LLC
Chambersburg PA
CBHW030941180526
45163CB00002B/656